The
Last
Frontier

The
Last
Frontier

An Analysis of the
Strategic Defense Initiative

Gary L. Guertner

AND

Donald M. Snow

Lexington Books

D.C. Heath and Company/Lexington, Massachusetts/Toronto

Library of Congress Cataloging in Publication Data

Guertner, Gary L.
Strategy and missile defense.

Includes index.
1. Strategic Defense Initiative.   I. Snow, Donald M.,
1943–   . II. Title.
UG743.G84   1986   358′.1754′0973   85-45923
ISBN 0-669-12370-6 (alk. paper)

Published simultaneously in Canada
Printed in the United States of America
Casebound International Standard Book Number: 0-669-12370-6
Library of Congress Catalog Card Number: 85-45923

The paper used in this publication meets the minimum requirements of
American National Standard for Information Sciences—Permanance of
Paper for Printed Library Materials, ANSI Z39.48-1984.

The last numbers on the right below indicate the number and date of
printing.

10   9   8   7   6   5   4   3   2

95   94   93   92   91   90   89   88   87

*To Brandon and Megan
and Rickey for making the effort worthwhile*

Contents

Figures and Tables

Figures

Tables

Preface

The search for security in the nuclear age periodically opens major policy debates that push us in new strategic directions. The president's March 1983 speech opened the newest round in those debates by bringing strategic defense research out of the laboratory, where it had progressed quietly for a decade, onto center stage with his political endorsement for a bold new space-based defense program that would "achieve our ultimate goal of eliminating the threat posed by strategic nuclear missiles." The "star wars" speech was not only born out of the technological advances being made in U.S. weapons laboratories. A critical ingredient was Reagan's deeply felt frustration over American vulnerability to mass destruction from a nuclear war, and the apparent inability of any president to regain or even attempt to regain control over our own security.

Subsequent speeches, congressional testimonies, press conferences, and commissioned study groups placed the Reagan administration on record as defining the Strategic Defense Initiative (*SDI*) as a research program with objectives that have been clearly delineated by the administration. SDI and its growing administrative and research infrastructure have been asked to solve a number of fundamental scientific and engineering problems. A future decision to deploy a partial or layered strategic defense system will depend on emerging technologies that are:

Technically achievable,

Effective against Soviet forces,

Affordable,

Survivable,

Cost-effective at the margin (Deploying additional increments of defense is cheaper than additional offensive countermeasures.),

Compatible with strategic stability.

This book examines whether and under what conditions these prudent, but difficult to achieve criteria can be met. The authors began their analyses of SDI independently. Their efforts have been joined in a single volume because of a shared sense of perplexity that the strategic defense debate was following well established and predictable ideological lines. Fundamental differences over how best to achieve and maintain a stable nuclear deterrent, and disagreements about the value of arms control have been projected into the strategic defense debate. Opponents come largely from the pro-arms control community and from among those who oppose deterrence based on what they see as destabilizing counterforce strategies and weapons. Proponents are drawn largely from the pro-defense modernization faction and those who favor deterrence strategies based on very detailed and flexible nuclear war fighting options and strategies.

Don Snow is slightly more optimistic about the future potential of SDI technologies and strategy than Gary Guertner, but fears program costs will confront strategic planners with formidable obstacles. Guertner focuses on the technical problems SDI proponents must overcome to achieve their strategic goals, the critical relationships between those technical successes and offensive arms control agreements during the transition to strategic defense, and the problems military strategists may have to confront in a defense-dominant world.

The authors clearly have their biases, but the mutual effort to pull one another toward objective, middle-ground positions, even if only partially successful, makes the book one of the few sources (perhaps the only source) that examines the issues of strategic defense without a purposeful effort to side with critics or proponents.

It is from these differing but ultimately compatible vantage points that *The Last Frontier* emerges. Chapter 1 provides an introduction and overview of the subject, discussing the general subject of defenses against missile attacks, the general arguments about the relationship between missile defenses and the nuclear goal of deterrence, and the general nature of the technologies generally subsumed under the prospects for SDI. The chapter concludes with a brief history of the Reagan administration's shifting attitude to the program.

Chapter 2 begins the more substantive discussion of SDI. On the assumption that some of the same arguments that enlivened the antiballistic missile (ABM) debate of the 1960s will also be present in the examination of SDI, it begins with a retrospective on the ABM, focusing on those factors which contributed to the repudiation of active defenses at that time. The chapter then addresses both the principal arguments that will be used for and against ballistic missile defense in the ongoing debate over SDI.

Chapter 3 cautions scientists and program administrators against self-deceiving optimism. Two specific issues are examined in detail. First is the methodological debate over how many space-based battle stations will be required for an effective layered defense. The second is the separate problems of evaluating the technical successes of individual components and the systematic reliability of strategic defenses under wartime conditions when all components must function as an integrated system against a determined adversary.

Chapter 4 describes strategic offensive–defensive relationships and how they are affected by both military strategy and arms control. An offensive arms control regime will be essential in meeting the goals of strategic defense, but negotiating strategies will become increasingly complex due to "gray area" weapons such as antisatellite weapons (ASATs) that may have both offensive and defensive capabilities.

Chapter 5 describes possible Soviet tactical adaptations to strategic defense in the absence of arms control. These include the massing of forces through additional deployments of fixed and mobile intercontinental ballistic missiles (ICBMs), circumvention of ballistic missile defenses by air- and sea-launched cruise missiles, and the deployment of more powerful and threatening conventional forces in the European theater.

Chapter 6 describes the irony of offensive doctrine in a defense-dominant world. It concludes that both sides may be driven to countercity targeting doctrines (aiming weapons at urban complexes) to compensate for the declining penetrability of their offensive forces.

In the concluding chapter the authors agree that strategic defense has popular appeal and is a worthy long-range research goal. In the short term, however, testing and development decisions may have to be sacrificed in favor of offensive arms reductions until a future political climate permits a cooperative Soviet–American transition to a defense-dominant world. This route offers the surest path to security by avoiding the pitfalls of unilateral efforts to find security in the nuclear age through unacceptable levels of technological dependency and untestable strategic systems.

As complex and technical as these issues are, they are too important and far reaching in their consequences for the debate to be monopolized by a small, technical/strategic elite. For that reason, the authors have attempted to write the book in a style that is comprehensible to the layman, but at a level of analysis to be of value to scholars and policy makers.

Most readers will find that the book raises as many questions as it answers. This is inevitable given the nature of a program still in its formative, research stages. The final answers and the ultimate burden of proof will fall decidedly on those new pioneers of strategic defense who must demonstrate that their vision will lead to a safer world.

The authors are grateful to former colleagues at the Army and Naval War Colleges, the U.S. Arms Control and Disarmament Agency, and the University of Alabama for their comments, insights, and steady determination to find solutions to the problems discussed in this book. Not all will agree with the arguments presented by the authors. All, however, share in whatever strengths the book may have.

The
Last
Frontier

1
The Road to the Strategic Defense Initiative

O n March 23, 1983, President Reagan surprised the nation by
announcing, in the midst of a broad-ranging speech, that he
had committed the United States to the spirited exploration of the
possibilities of developing a space-based defense against nuclear-
armed ballistic missiles. In his pleading with the scientific community to engage in a crash program of research akin to that which
created the first atomic bomb, the president held out the long-term
hope for ending the so-called "reign of nuclear terror" initiated by
the successful combining of nuclear bombs and ballistic missiles.
The administration quickly dubbed the entire effort the Strategic
Defense Initiative (SDI), while critics derisively called it "Star
Wars."

The major effect of the president's action was to reopen the national debate over strategic nuclear defenses which had lain essentially fallow since the signing of the Anti-Ballistic Missile Treaty in
1972. That agreement, widely designated the centerpiece of SALT
I, had effectively precluded the possibility that either the Soviet
Union or the United States could deploy missile defenses that would
have any real effect in blunting an attack on one another. A defense
intellectual community, dominated at the time by supporters of the
strategic nuclear strategy of assured destruction, applauded and
pronounced strategic defense dead and their preferred strategy (in
which defenselessness is a central tenet) as triumphant.

The celebration was, of course, premature. To paraphrase Mark
Twain's famous quotation, announcements of the death of ballistic

missile defense (BMD) were greatly exaggerated. By establishing very low limits on the number of ABMs allowable, the treaty only guaranteed that such systems would be impotent against a concerted attack.[1] What the treaty did not do was ban research and development activity short of the observable and hence verifiable level of systems and major subsystems testing. The effect of allowing R&D to continue was to permit the supporters of BMD to retire from the congressional and diplomatic battlefields bloodied but unbroken to the sanctity and privacy of their laboratories to prepare for a better day. To their chagrin, when the president made his announcement, the opponents of BMD had not won as much as they thought when they achieved their victory in the ABM Treaty.

One of the initiatives going on in the weapons laboratories was the investigation of the weapons possibilities of a group of new physical principles known collectively as directed energy transfer (DET) weapons. The most prominent of those DET technologies were high-energy lasers (HEL) and charged-particle beams (CPB), and among the more obvious possible military applications of these technologies was strategic defense. President Carter, through Secretary of Defense Harold Brown, had a Directed Energy Transfer Office established within the research arm of the Department of Defense, and the initiative, especially regarding space-based lasers, was continued by the Reagan administration when it entered office in 1981.

Efforts in this area were being reported in the public literature as well. *Aviation Week and Space Technology,* that semiofficial journal that acts as a conduit for leaking information about government activities in the aerospace area, began discussing the DET area on a regular basis as early as the middle 1970s.[2]

What this suggests is that anyone who was paying attention had no reason to be caught off guard by the SDI. Many analysts, particularly those outside government, were, of course, surprised by this dramatic and forceful reappearance of an interest in ballistic missile defense, and professed great horror and amazement that the issue, which they had supposedly killed in 1972, would reemerge. What they mainly demonstrated was their inattention to a decade's worth of developments going on inside U.S. weapons laboratories.

The SDI debate is highly contentious and is likely to remain so for the foreseeable future for at least two reasons. The first is that the technologies that individually and collectively comprise the effort are in an incomplete, developmental status that makes it impossible to predict with great assurance exactly what the enterprise's fruit (or its absence) will be. SDI could produce a perfect defense, no defense, or something in between, and no one can know for sure which at this juncture.

This first cause for contention is endemic and unavoidable until the total scientific evidence is in. The second source of contention, however, is not entirely unavoidable. That source is public and even expert confusion over exactly what the SDI proposal is and what it pretends to produce. There is confusion over the issue partly because well intentioned observers do not understand it thoroughly and clearly. But there is more. At the same time, SDI has become the current lightning rod in the entire strategic debate over preferred means to enhance deterrence. On the one hand, many of the advocacies and oppositions are really statements about preferred nuclear strategies where the principals, unfortunately, do not always admit that it is a deterrent theology that they are seeking to buttress and reinforce. On the other hand, advocates and opponents are engaged in a kind of literary and verbal guerrilla warfare over SDI that is an extension of the skirmishes of the 1970s.

The victim, in either case, is clear and dispassionate analysis of missile defense generally and the SDI specifically. What is needed is an analysis that is not self-interested and that can look at the entire concern in perspective. This is the task that this book, at least in a tentative way, seeks to accomplish.

The remainder of this chapter seeks to begin that pursuit by creating some sense of context for the discussion of the SDI proposal. To accomplish that end, we will do four things. First, the entire conceptual context of defenses against nuclear attack will be presented, emphasizing where the SDI proposals fit in. Second, the positions of the various schools of thought about nuclear deterrence on missile defenses will be explored, since many advocacies and oppositons to SDI are basically extensions of those broader beliefs. Third, a brief discussion of the basic scientific dynamics of the technologies that make up DET weaponry will be presented as a kind of primer for more detailed and technical concerns. Fourth and finally, the chapter will conclude with a brief excursion through the various steps the administration took in the process of its conversion to the cause of strategic defense, SDI-style.

Nuclear Defenses

Although the dominance of offensive weapons over defensive weapons has been a hallmark of the nuclear age, the prospect of trying successfully to defend against a nuclear attack has never been absent. Before the advent of the ballistic missile as the primary method for delivering nuclear warheads to their targets, conventional defenses (that is, antiaircraft defenses) offered the possibility of deflecting some sizeable proportion of an attacking force, thereby rendering the effect of such an attack bearable by some calculations.

The ballistic missile seemed permanently to change such calculations. Because ballistic missiles travel at speeds of up to 15,000 miles per hour, there appeared to be no practical method to stop an attack once launched, so that the entire enterprise had to revolve around deterrence—assuring that the attack never occurred in the first place.

As depicted in table 1–1, there are two basic types of defense that might be used against a nuclear (or for that matter, nonnuclear) attack that can, in turn, be used to protect two types of target. The two kinds of defense are labelled passive and active, with passive defenses further subdivided into evasive and absorptive techniques. Targets that might be protected are labelled counterforce or countervalue, using conventional terminology.

Passive defenses, as the name implies, do not seek to deflect an attack by trying to destroy incoming weapons; instead, they defend by lessening the effects that the weapons have on the target. This is accomplished in one of two ways, either by making the target moveable and thus difficult to find and destroy (through evasive techniques) or by making the target more resistant to the weapon's effects (through absorptive techniques). Active defenses, on the other hand, seek to protect by attacking and either destroying or disabling the incoming weapon before it can reach its target.

Two categories of target are generally defined as the objects that these defenses might protect. These are counterforce targets, (military or militarily useful targets) and countervalue targets (the things

Table 1–1
Defense Options

DEFENSE OPTIONS

	PASSIVE DEFENSE		ACTIVE DEFENSE
	Evasive	Absorptive	
COUNTERFORCE TARGETS	Mobility	Hardening	Point Defense
COUNTERVALUE TARGETS	Evacuation	Shelters	Area Defense

people value). Counterforce targets are further divided into so-called time-sensitive and non-time-sensitive categories, where the basis of differentiation is whether or not the target (which is a weapon) must be destroyed very rapidly to avoid its being fired at you. Missile silos are a good example of a time-sensitive target, while an army post would be a non-time-sensitive target. The best example of a countervalue target, of course, is a city.

These distinctions can be combined in matrix form, as table 1–1 does, to see the possible forms that defense can take. Evasive passive techniques for defending counterforce targets, for instance, include such actions as hardening missile silos so that they can withstand anything but a direct hit (where the silo is part of the crater created by the explosion) or placing command bunkers well underground. Passive evasive techniques for counterforce targets encompass the various means of making weapons systems mobile and hence untargetable. The nuclear-missile-carrying submarine is the prime example of this technique, as are bomber alert and scramble procedures as well as proposals for a land-based mobile missile (the Midgetman).

The passive techniques for protecting counterforce targets are generally well established and accepted as beneficial, although silo-hardening has come under some question as Soviet warheads become increasingly accurate. Applying these same kinds of techniques to defending population has been highly controversial, because of costs and the many uncertainties in protecting our population centers from both the immediate and long-range effects of a nuclear war.

Passive countervalue protection falls under the generic category of civil defense, and civil defense plans developed by the Federal Emergency Management Agency (FEMA) incorporate both evasive and absorptive plans. Evacuation of urban populations to so-called rural "host areas" is the major evasive technique, whereas the system of designated blast and radiation shelters is the primary absorptive method.

The chief source of controversy about passive countervalue defenses is over whether they would have any salutary effects. When John Kennedy first urged Americans to provide for their self-protection in 1961, thousands of Americans had their backyards dug up and shelters installed. In 1985, few people know the evacuation plan for themselves and their community or have any earthly idea where the shelter is located to which they should repair in the event of an emergency. The simple fact is that most Americans do not take civil defense against nuclear attack seriously, despite the attempts by some in the Reagan administration (notably T. K. Jones in the Defense Department) to revive interest in FEMA.

Active defenses fall under the category of ballistic missile defenses. Air defenses are also part of the consideration conceptually, but have not, in the United States anyway, been a serious part of the concern. The major reason for this omission has been the Soviet lack of interest in strategic-range bomber aircraft. Recent Soviet development of longer-range bombers such as BACKFIRE and BLACKJACK, combined with advances in cruise missile technology, are likely to force air defenses back into the overall assessment of U.S. defense requirements as would, ironically, the development of effective ballistic missile defenses. BMD would be useful against a missile attack but probably irrelevant in attacking manned and unmanned aircraft. For the moment, however, the chief concern is with BMD.

Missile defenses can attempt to protect either populations

(countervalue targets) or counterforce targets. Of the two, protecting population is both the more demanding and more controversial. It is more demanding because a defense of population must be essentially foolproof (what is known in the jargon as leakproof) to be useful at all. Given the destructive power of thermonuclear weapons, a defense that does not intercept everything hurled at a population center would still result in tremendous death and suffering. The performance criterion for these "area" defenses (so called because they must protect large physical areas) is thus absolute: they must work perfectly to be desirable.

Not everyone agrees with this designation. Some analysts propose that even a partially effective population defense would be of value because it would mean more Americans would survive an attack and thus be able to speed recovery from the disaster. While this line of analysis has value, its chief limitation is that one can never specify in advance who or how many would survive, making the expenditure of scarce public resources a dubious proposition in purely political terms.

The performance criterion for protecting counterforce targets is more lenient. The chief examples of such target are land-based retaliatory forces, such as ICBMs. Any extent to which additional retaliatory forces are saved by a defense is valuable, since each additional missile adds to the retaliatory fury available after an attack, the prospect of which is what purports to deter in the first place. Because of this, the criterion for counterforce defense is said to be incremental—the better it works, the better it is.

Ballistic missile defenses can also be categorized in terms of the technologies they employ. The most familiar technique is the so-called antiballistic missile. The basis of this technology is to use one ballistic missile to attack another. Once a launch has been sighted, the ABM is dispatched so that what Robert Jastrow refers to as the "smart bullet" in its tip reaches a point in space or the upper atmosphere at the same time as the attacking reentry vehicle (RV).[3] Using either a nuclear or nonnuclear explosive, the ABM explodes, destroying or disabling the attacking weapon.

The chief drawback of ABMs is speed. The ABM travels at roughly the same speed as the attacking weapon, meaning that it cannot literally catch up to the target. Rather, one is forced to lead the incoming RV by calculating an interception point somewhere in flight. If the RV has, for instance, the ability to alter its trajectory, it can elude the defender, while even a slight miscalculation can render the ABM ineffective. This kind of problem is what led John Kennedy to describe the problem of missile defense as akin to shooting a bullet with another bullet.

There is a second set of technologies for active missile defense. These encompass directed energy transfer, and have returned strategic defense to the agenda. Although the operation of these systems is discussed somewhat more fully in a later section, all the DET technologies potentially work on the principle of projecting an intensive beam of either laser light or radiation onto a rising missile either during its boost phase, in midflight, or in reentry. The chief advantage that these prospects have over ABMs is that, especially in the case of lasers, they travel at the speed of light, much faster than the attacking missile or reentry vehicle, allowing for an instant attack directly against the offensive weapon.

Of the two forms of BMD, ABM defenses are much closer to reality, and proponents such as retired Lt. General Daniel Graham and Jastrow maintain that an effective defense could be mounted in the next few years using readily available ABM designs.[4] The so-called "exotic" DET technologies that comprise the most visible elements of the SDI, on the other hand, are all in the reasonably early developmental stage. Some component testing has begun, as was announced as part of one of the space shuttle missions in summer 1985, but the development and testing of major subsystems and systems are somewhere off in the future; very few maintain that any of these will become available until sometime in the early 2000s.

These distinctions create the context for discussing defense against nuclear attack. Generally speaking, defense of counterforce targets has had greater acceptance in the American debate, largely on the grounds of effectiveness. Passive countervalue defense has generally been treated as a will-of-the-wisp not worthy of serious consideration because of its impracticality. To some extent, active defenses have shared in this suspicion about their practicality. At the same time, the preference that different advocates have for different nuclear strategies of deterrence also color their views on the desirability of nuclear defense.

Ballistic Missile Defense and Deterrence

Broadly speaking, the nuclear debate over what strategies most enhance deterrence began in earnest in the wake of Sputnik and the ICBM. This factor is of symbolic importance in considering nuclear defenses, because it means the debate was framed by the presumed impossibility of self-defense against nuclear attack.

As the debate has evolved in the American context, it has attached to two poles. These poles, in turn, revolve on the question of whether a nuclear war, once started, could be limited, which in turn colors perceptions about what best maintains the deterrent condition in the first place.

One pole in the debate, of course, is preference for the strategy of assured destruction. Proponents of assured destruction, either explicitly or implicitly, start from the assumption that a nuclear war once begun would create such passions and emotions that it would inexorably devolve to an all-out, unlimited exchange that would be catastrophic to all concerned. Because of this, deterrence is the prime, possibly sole, value, and it is activated by making the consequences of deterrence failing so appalling that no one will let that occur.

The chief threat underlying AD is the prospect of an unacceptable, assured destruction retaliation in the event of a Soviet strike. The Soviets, aware of the consequences of their transgression, are deterred because they are, in effect, hostages to American retaliatory fury. As a result, they do not attack in the first place.

In this scheme, missile defenses are doctrinally undesirable. Since the secret to deterrence under assured destruction is absolute assurance that the price of aggression is death and destruction, any capability that might make that assured destruction seem less certain is viewed as destabilizing and undesirable, because it potentially lowers inhibitions and makes the hostages feel free.

What this means in particular is that assured destruction adherents are opposed in principle to active defenses against countervalue targets, since such defenses attack the hostage principle on which their strategic preference rests. Protecting counterforce targets is not doctrinally odious, on the other hand, because any protection provided for retaliatory forces simply increases the fury available for retribution and thus strengthens the deterrent effects. As a practical matter, however, most assured destruction adherents oppose counterforce defense as well, because they fear it to be the Trojan horse for more general defenses, including the doctrinally objectionable defense of population.

The other pole in the debate revolves around the notion that nuclear war can be limited, or at least that one should make plans and efforts to limit its extent. This belief (or hope) is associated with the strategy variously known as limited nuclear options, the countervailing strategy, and controlled reponse. The basis of this strategy was established in the early 1970s and continues to evolve under the Reagan administration. Given the known atrocity of all-out nuclear hostilities, more measured, or limited, forms of exchange are by definition the more likely forms nuclear war would take and thus form the real problem for deterrence. To meet those challenges, one needs a whole range of limited countermeasures that are appropriate to various forms of nuclear transgressions. If the Soviets recognize that the United States has appropriate countermeasures, they will hence be deterred.

The emphasis here is on what best deters and, should deterrence fail, how to limit the extent of the ensuing catastrophe. LNOs assume nuclear war might last for a time and consist of measured applications of nuclear power. As a result, and combined with the goal of mitigating the disaster, proponents of limited nuclear options are doctrinally positively disposed to the defense. Any active defense could provide endurability over sustained operations across time and limit the casualties from the war.

There is yet a third way to look at the deterrence that is emerging, at least implicitly, in the literature. This position starts from the first assumption that it is the first and paramount foreign policy priority of both the Soviet Union and the United States to avoid nuclear war with one another. This priority on both sides does not emerge from any sense of mutual love or even necessarily humanity, but from the stark recognition of the consequences of nuclear war. Given the assessment that such a conflict would be catastrophic, it is to be avoided at all costs.[5]

If this position is correct, and the weight of declaratory evidence by both sides certainly supports it, then the problem of deterrence changes. Conventional deterrence thought assumes hostile intentions that might be carried out in the absence of deterrence threats. Thus, the debate over assured destruction and limited nuclear options is essentially a disagreement over what kind of retaliatory threat deters aggression that the Soviets might carry out in the absence of the threat.

The third perspective, however, says this debate is essentially irrelevant, because the superpowers are effectively self-deterred by their fear of the consequences of nuclear war. Mutual fear, and not intentions that require dissuasion, is the dynamic of deterrence. This position can be called realistic self-deterrence.

From this perspective, the deterrence problem is narrowed. With the presumption of aggressive intention removed as the primary dynamic to be contained, the problem becomes maintenance of the condition where self-deterrence occurs. This seems to create two requirements for the deterrence systems.

The first is crisis management and avoidance if nuclear war will not occur because of a purposive decision by one side or another to launch it, then it can only start by inadvertence. The major situation where that could occur would be if a crisis (either begun between the superpowers or initiated by a third party or parties) got out of hand. Thus, actions which assist in the avoidance of crises or which allow crises to be contained and defused at the least dangerous levels become a primary goal for maintaining deterrence stability.

The second priority is to maintain a weapons balance where neither side can recalculate the unacceptability of nuclear exchange. This is a question of relative arsenal balances and a problem to which arms control is clearly relevant.

Missile defenses are basically compatible with this approach. Clearly, BMD assists in crisis management, since the degree of effectiveness of a BMD system lowers proportionately any incentives to initiate hostilities to avoid the consequences of the adversary's counterforce capability. If both sides field limited and survivable offensive forces and active defenses that are more or less symmetrical in capability (a problem dealt with in chapter 2), then alternations in relative balances are unlikely to occur either, meeting the second priority. What this discussion suggests is that advocacy or opposition to missile defenses, and more specifically the SDI, is grounded not entirely in assessments about the likely effectiveness of this particular proposal; it is also conditioned by more general convictions about what deters best. Often, it is difficult to determine in any individual statement of support or opposition which kind of judgment is actually being stated. The strategic defense debate also requires a basic understanding of the kinds of technologies under investigation, to which the discussion now turns.

SDI Technologies

For advocates and critics alike, there are justifiable concerns about the unprecedented technological dependency SDI would bring to U.S. security. The president and other proponents of the Strategic Defense Initiative are quick to point out that the entire effort at this juncture is no more than a research endeavor aimed at exploring the defensive potential of various technologies. Accepting that assertion at face value, the kinds of technologies under investigation and the general directions and purposes of those investigations have been underway for a decade or more and have been a matter of the public record for nearly that long. This public record allows at least some general discussion.

Two technologies, collectively falling under the category of directed energy transfer weapons, comprise the SDI. The first and most highly publicized of these technologies involves the laser beam. As a strategic defensive weapon, basing lasers in space is the most commonly discussed possibility. The other technology involves charged-particle beams, either in space (exoatmospheric) or on earth (endoatmospheric).

A laser is a highly focused and concentrated beam of light. The word laser is an acronym standing for light amplified by stimulated emission of radiation. In practice, a laser involves propogating a focused light beam, passing it through a gaseous medium which enhances its power and focus, and then directing it at some object through mirrors and lenses. Because a laser is a beam of light, it is subject to the normal atmospheric conditions that affect any light beam, such as defraction and diffusion. Because these sources can degrade the effectiveness of the beam, it becomes attractive to base a laser weapon in space, where atmospheric degrading influences are absent.

A laser based in space has two basic advantages in attacking offensive missiles. First, it can travel over very long distances (for example, thousands of miles) without being appreciably degraded. Second, the beam travels at the speed of light, which means it moves much faster than the missile it seeks to attack and can locate and attack that missile essentially instantly without the need to lead the object (as is the problem for conventional ABMs).

A laser can attack and destroy or disable an offensive weapon in one of three ways. First, it can focus a hot beam on the delicate "skin" of a missile, either burning a hole in the missile or weakening its structure, which causes the missile to self-destruct. Second, the force of the laser as it hits the missile can knock it slightly off course, causing it to miss its target. Third, the effect of the laser can disrupt the delicate guidance or fusing electronics of the reentry vehicle, thereby causing the mechanism to malfunction. Any of these effects can serve the defensive purpose.

There are several problems in developing laser defenses, three of which are worth mentioning here. The first is propogating a sufficiently powerful laser to accomplish the mission. This is a problem of both the kind of laser that is used and the power requirements to generate it. Since the laser would be on a satellite (or laser station), it is necessary to develop a power source that is economical in size, weight, and refueling requirements. The second problem is effectiveness of a coordinated system to intercept a massive Soviet launch. Intercepting fourteen hundred rockets simultaneously rising from their silos is an operational problem calling for extreme coordination and efficiency that has, among other things, mind-boggling cybernetic requirements. The third problem, discussed more fully in a later chapter, is possible countermeasures that the Soviets might mount.

None of these problems is trivial. The power source and machinery of current designs that would propagate a sufficiently powerful beam for missile interception weigh tons (though scientists disagree about how many). The weights involved would tax even the space shuttle, especially when refueling requirements are taken into account. As a result of this difficulty (and the prospect that the laser station itself might be vulnerable to attack), there is a proposal to base the actual laser propagator on the Earth and to beam up the laser into space, where the satellites would serve as mirrors to redirect the laser beam to target. Likewise, the system's effectiveness against a massive attack will never be realistically simulated in advance of an actual attack, and there are a variety of countermeasures that may be possible against lasers, some of which are relatively economical.

The other technology associated with the SDI is the charged-particle beam. This technology is similar to the laser in that it operates on the principle of transferring energy from one surface to another via a beam; the two differ in that the energy transferred from a laser is in the form of concentrated light, while the particle beam consists of concentrated subatomic particles in the form of radiation. For strategic applications, particle beam research is in its relative infancy. The theoretical problem that has bedeviled those seeking to apply particle beam research to missile defense is what kind of beam is most effective and amenable to the mission.

The answer appears to be the neutral-particle beam, which gets its name because the subatomic particles that form the beam are fast neutrons and gamma rays that have no electrical charge (and hence are neutral). The problem has been how to propagate a sufficiently disciplined reaction to allow such a beam to be formed and to travel across space. Only recently has such work been attempted successfully.

If the technological problems can be solved the neutral-particle beam holds the promise of being the most effective of the DET technologies. It has considerable advantages over particle beams using positively or negatively charged particles, because such beams are subject to diffusion, dispersion, and gravity, whereas a neutral beam is essentially immune to all those effects.

The neutral beam also has distinct potential advantages over lasers, for at least two reasons. The first is that such beams can operate on earth as well as in space, because the influences that degrade a light beam apparently do not affect them. Thus, the problem of the weight of the propagator is diminished. Second, the neutral-particle beam works on the principle of penetrating the missile at which it is aimed with highly radioactive particles that scramble and destroy the electronic guidance and detonating mechanisms, thereby rendering them useless. This bombardment is apparently not subject to effective countermeasures, because sheathing (the most effective countermeasure) would add so much weight to the rocket as to make it virtually unlaunchable. Research and development on both lasers and particle beams is in its relatively rudimentary stages, and there are serious obstacles to be overcome before a weapon or weapon prototype will be produced. It is, for instance, one thing scientifically to produce a laser beam the size of a pencil, and quite another to produce a similar beam a meter or more in diameter (the size probably necessary for missile interception). Moreover, the research currently underway is on components of the systems that could become weapons, not on the total systems. Whether the components and the systems constructed from those components will produce workable missile defenses is still an open scientific and engineering question.

This is all to say that the SDI is still a scientific concept that is unproven. At least as a concept and prospect, however, the Reagan administration has adopted the SDI as its vision of a preferable strategic future. How the administration came to this determination is the subject of the final section of this chapter.

The Reagan Genesis

The rebirth of official interest in strategic defense was the result of many forces. The star wars speech represented a conjunction of political, military, philosophical, and technical forces that had been struggling for many years toward a common goal of ending or at least modifying the nation's reliance on offensive nuclear retaliation for its security from Soviet attack. Few strategic concepts have had so profound an impact on policy in so short a period of time. From the president's Star Wars speech to renewed Soviet–American arms control negotiations a year later, strategic defense became both the centerpiece and philosophical foundation for long-range strategic planning and arms control policies.

As early as his unsuccessful 1976 presidential campaign, Reagan had questioned U.S. strategic nuclear policies. He often compared them to two men pointing pistols at each other's head. The pistols were his metaphor for the immense offensive arsenals of the United States and the Soviet Union. He often told aides there has to be a better way.

In 1980, during the Republican presidential primary campaign, Mr. Reagan discussed a NORAD (North American Air Defense) briefing with journalist Robert Sheer. General James Hill, then commander-in-chief of NORAD, had, Sheer explained, demonstrated NORAD's ability to track countless objects in space and provide early warning of attacks against the continental United States. Reagan responded that it seemed ironic that our technology can do all of these things, yet we cannot stop any of the weapons that are coming at us. "I don't think there's been a time in history when there wasn't a defense against some kind of thrust, even back in the old-fashion days when we had coast artillery that would stop invading ships."[6]

The president's sentiments and frustrations were attuned to the Republican party platform, which called for "vigorous research and development of an effective antiballistic missile system." (The platform also called for new offensive missiles and overall military and technologic superiority over the Soviet Union.) Reagan's inclinations were also reinforced through numerous policy memoranda and position papers he received early in the campaign. For example, Martin Anderson, a senior fellow at the conservative Hoover Institution at Stanford University, wrote in a memo on foreign and defense policy that it was time to seriously reconsider antiballistic missile constraints. In a prescient passage Anderson wrote that such an idea "is probably fundamentally far more appealing to the American people than the questionable satisfaction of knowing that those who initiated an attack against us were also blown away."[7]

Wyoming Senator Malcolm Wallop also gave Reagan a lengthy proballistic missile defense article he had prepared for publication. Reagan responded that he too wanted to make strategic defense an issue in the campaign. Reagan's political advisers winced, however, at the idea of their candidate talking about lasers, space weapons, abrogation of the ABM Treaty, or radical change in strategic doctrine at a time when the press was filled with Rube Goldberg characterizations of the Carter MX basing proposals (shuttling the giant missile between protected shelters). A campaign version of the Star Wars speech might have been too much for the American public. Instead, the campaign and the first two years of Reagan's presidency focused on the strategic modernization of offensive nuclear weapons and an across-the-board build-up of U.S. military capabilities.

Others outside the administration continued to advance the concept of strategic defense. The conservative Heritage Foundation published *High Frontier,* a study directed by retired army general Daniel O. Graham. Heritage lobbying and the pleadings of many aerospace industry engineers sparked congressional interest.

Research at the weapons laboratories, most notably Livermore and Sandia, was progressing in exotic new lasers and particle beam technologies—"third generation" weapons in the words of Edward Teller. For decades Teller had been interested in technologies that could defend the United States from Soviet nuclear weapons. If third generation weapons were feasible, they could free the country from the legacy of Hiroshima which Teller had helped create in the New Mexico desert.

These technological developments were watched closely by a group of influential scientists, aerospace executives, and retired military officers who began to meet in Washington, D.C., at the Heritage Foundation. Their common goal was to formulate a plan for creating a national system of defense. The group split, however, over projects that would require long-term research and those, such as General Graham's high frontier concept, that could be deployed sooner on the basis of near-term technology.

Graham expounded his concept in language remarkably similar to that used in the president's announcement. The high frontier plan would replace the "ludicrous notion" of deterrence by mutual assured destruction with the concept of "assured survival." By providing strategic defenses, the high frontier system would render the intercontinental ballistic missile "practically obsolete." Graham's concepts for ballistic missile defenses based on more rapidly deployable technology were, however, rejected after extensive review by the Pentagon. Secretary of Defense Weinberger was unwilling early in the administration to commit the nation to a course which called for capabilities that did not currently exist.

The "long-term" research faction headed by Karl R. Bendetson, long-time overseer of the Hoover Institution, gained the president's ear, and Bendetson met with him on three occasions in 1982, prior to the star wars speech.[8] Teller met with the president as part of that group and he also met privately with Reagan in September 1982, when he assured the president that the new technologies would challenge the widespread notion that practical defenses could not be obtained.[9]

Outsiders who supported ballistic missile defense had the president's ear, but insiders, especially in the Department of Defense, were more interested in offensive nuclear weapons and the president's strategic modernization programs. These, after all, had been the basis of his campaign theme to reverse the decline of American military power. Indeed, the road to SDI might be titled a tale of two speeches if we look closely at the dramatic and far-reaching shifts the president made between his strategic modernization speech on October 2, 1981, and his star wars speech of March 23, 1983.

The president's strategic modernization speech marked the fulfillment of his campaign pledge to halt the decline in America's military strength and restore the margin of safety needed for the protection of the American people. His program required major funding in five categories:

1. Construction of 100 B-1 bombers and development of the advanced technology or "stealth" bomber,
2. Continued construction of Trident submarines and the development of the D-5 missile,
3. Completion of the MX missile (limited by Congress to 50 as of 1985),
4. Rebuilding of command, communications, and control systems,
5. Greater investment in air defense and civil defense.

These strategic modernization programs centered on improving the credibility of U.S. deterrence policies through strengthening offensive capabilities. On the strategic defense side, only air defense and civil defense programs were singled out in the president's speech. Ballistic missile defense was not mentioned, although research programs continued at levels near those of the Carter administration.

Against the backdrop of the perennially troubled MX missile and the perceived erosion of strategic stability due to the continuing Soviet military build-up, the president met with the Joint Chiefs of Staff. This particular meeting in February, 1983, may have been pivotal. Admiral James D. Watkins, Chief of Naval Operations, with the encouragement of then-deputy national security affairs advisor Robert C. McFarlane, argued on moral grounds that Reagan should abandon the old doctrine of mutual assured destruction. A second argument that caught Reagan's attention was the Joint Chiefs' agreement that technology had improved sufficiently to make it worthwhile to proceed with research on defensive systems. Armed with Watkins's moral imperative, which matched his own, and the Joint Chiefs' optimism (on technology, but not necessarily on strategic defense per se), the president was ready to proceed promptly.

He was scheduled to give a nationally televised speech seeking support for the MX missile and the defense budget. While Chief of Staff James Baker was preparing the speech, McFarlane secretly drafted an insert to the speech which aides called "MX-plus."[10] Had then-national security advisor William Clark or McFarlane circulated the idea through normal interagency review, objections from virtually all the major players—the office of the Secretary of Defense, the Joint Chiefs, the State Department, the Arms Control and Disarmament Agency—might have killed it in much the same fashion as Weinberger killed high frontier. Instead, ideas building up in the president's mind from many sources came to a climax in the February meeting with the Joint Chiefs, who seemed to play the role of legitimizers on both moral and technical grounds. The Chiefs believed they were engaging the president in a broad background conversation. There is no evidence to suggest that they were aware that their remarks might contribute to a sudden and dramatic shift in American strategic priorities. Nevertheless, vague ideas and faith in American scientific virtuosity were translated into a firm statement of policy on a "close-hold" basis inside the White House.

The star wars insert was delivered on March 23, 1983. It caught Washington by surprise in what science advisor George Keyworth described later as a demonstration of "top-down leadership." It is no wonder the president could tell *Newsweek*'s Morton Kandracke that he had thought of the idea himself. His mind had indeed been open and receptive to the flood of prostrategic defense arguments he had been exposed to for the previous three years. The president was now ready to challenge traditional wisdom about the basis of Soviet–American mutual deterrence.

The president's proposal was followed by a flurry of official and unofficial studies, articles, congressional hearings, diplomatic cables, and speeches. All emphasized that the Strategic Defense Initiative was a research program and not a decision to deploy strategic defenses. That decision lay far in the future. For the present, SDI's fate was turned over to two major study groups initiated by National Security Study Directive (NSSD) 6-83. The most important was the technological study group (the Defensive Technologies Study Team or Fletcher Panel), which produced a seven-volume study concluding that some new technologies looked promising in their potential applications to missile defense, provided Soviet offensive countermeasures could be constrained and the problem of vulnerable space-based components alleviated.

The Fletcher Panel urged that a vigorous research and development program, broadly based but highly goal-oriented, be pursued. These efforts would permit informed decisions on whether to initiate, in the early 1990s, an engineering validation phase leading to a deployed defensive capability after the year 2000. Certain intermediate technologies could and should be demonstrated as part of the evolutionary R&D program. The panel further noted that the potential existed for earlier, phased deployment against constrained threats. The panel's report implicitly required the continuation of an arms control regime to meet cost and technical requirements for ballistic missile defense.

The Future Security Strategy Study Group or Hoffman Study Group examined the role of defenses in U.S. security policy. This group concluded:

> Deployment of defensive systems can increase stability, but to attain this we must design our offensive and defensive forces properly—and, especially, we must not allow them to be vulnerable. In combination with other measures, defense can contribute to reducing the prelaunch vulnerability of our offensive forces. To increase stability, defenses must themselves avoid high vulnerabil-

ity, must be robust in the face of the enemy technical or tactical countermeasures, and must compete favorably in cost terms with expansion of the Soviet offensive force. A defense that was highly effective for an attack below some threshold but lost effectiveness very rapidly for larger attacks might decrease stability if super-imposed on vulnerable offensive systems.[11]

The Hoffman Study group was less explicit than the Fletcher Panel in requiring the continuation of an arms control regime in some form, but did stress the strategic importance of limiting Soviet attack capabilities. The study also referred to the defense competing favorably in cost terms with Soviet offensive forces, as well as to technical and tactical measures that might be undertaken to reduce the vulnerabilities of both offensive and defensive weapons.

These "summer studies," especially the Defensive Technologies Study, served as the general guides for implementing the Strategic Defense Initiative through a newly created Strategic Defense Initiative Organization (SDIO). SDIO's charter, a Department of Defense directive dated April 24, 1984, gave it broad responsibility under the Secretary of Defense to pursue research, coordinate and control various defense-related programs that had previously been frag-mented among the various services, defend the programs before Congress, and make specific recommendations to the Secretary of Defense. In creating SDIO, the Secretary of Defense directed that the Strategic Defense Initiative Program(SDIP):

Follow the technology plan identified by the Fletcher Panel and the policy approach outlined in the Hoffman Study,

Be carried out with full consultation with U.S. allies,

Place principal emphasis on nonnuclear technologies (research on other concepts being to provide contingency options),

Aim at producing a layered defense system that can be deployed in such a way as to increase the contribution of defenses to deterrence,

Protect U.S. options for near-term deployments of limited bal-listic missile defense.[12]

Lt. General James Abrahamson, former director of the space shuttle program, was appointed SDIO's first director, presiding over a vastly increased budget over previous allotments for SDI-related programs—$1.4 billion for the program's first year (FY85)—and seeking a $26 billion budget through FY89.

In a period of only thirteen months, philosophy, appropriated funds, and bureaucracy coalesced into what may become the most ambitious and difficult research and development program in the history of American defense policy. This book is aimed at the participants in the SDI, those who are concerned observers on the outside, and concerned Americans who are simply trying to comprehend the debate that strategic defense has created. The authors have attempted to raise the critical questions that must be answered before security becomes dependent on ballistic missile defenses. The answers to these questions are not entirely technical. Many of the most crucial challenges will be in the areas of military strategy and diplomacy—most specifically, they will be in the arena of offensive arms negotiations.

Notes

1. As amended by the 1974 Protocol, the ABM Treaty limits the United States and the U.S.S.R. to one ABM site of one hundred interceptors and one hundred launchers either around the national capital or an intercontinental ballistic missile field. The Soviet Union deployed and later modernized its ABM site around Moscow. The United States constructed and later deactivated its ABM site near an ICBM field in North Dakota.
2. The principal author of the *Aviation Week and Space Technology* series has been Clarence A. Robinson, Jr. His first accounts appeared in about 1977, and he has reported on developments in this area regularly ever since. See also Donald M. Snow, "Lasers, Charged-Particle Beams and the Strategic Future," *Political Science Quarterly* 95, no. 2 (Summer 1980):277–94 and "Over the Strategic Horizon: Directed Energy Transfer Weapons and Arms Control," *Arms Control Today* 9, no. 10 (November 1979): 1, 8–9.
3. Robert Jastrow, *How to Make Nuclear Weapons Obsolete* (Boston, Mass.: Little, Brown, 1985), pp. 91–92.
4. Daniel O. Graham and Gregory A. Fossedal, *A Defense That Defends: Blocking Nuclear Attack* (Old Greenwich, Conn.: Devin–Adair Publishers, 1983), pp. 44–45.
5. This general perspective is represented in Robert Kennedy, "The Changing Strategic Balance and U.S. Defense Planning" in *The Defense of the West:*

Strategic and European Security Issues Reappraised, ed. Robert Kennedy and John M. Weinstein (Boulder, Colo.: Westview Press, 1984), pp. 5–38. It is also reflected in the late Herman Kahn's posthumous work *Thinking about the Unthinkable in the 1980s* (New York: Simon and Schuster, 1984).

6. *New York Times,* March 4, 1985, p. A1.
7. *Washington Post,* March 3, 1985, p. 19.
8. *New York Times, op. cit.*
9. Discussion with one of the authors, September 28, 1982.
10. A National Security Council staffer, Colonel Allan Myer, drafted the president's speech. The insert was prepared by Robert McFarlane and Admiral John Poindexter.
11. Fred S. Hoffman, *Ballistic Missile Defenses and U.S. National Security: Summary Report,* prepared for the Future Security Strategy Study, Department of Defense, October 1983, p. 12.
12. *Strategic Defense Initiative Organization Charter,* Department of Defense memorandum, April 24, 1984, pp. 1–2.

2
The Prospects for Strategic Defense

As somewhat suggested in the introductory chapter, the question of whether the SDI is an attractive strategic and policy option depends to a large degree on the attitudes one has toward active defenses against nuclear-tipped missiles. One dimension of that question was discussed in chapter 1 with regard to how adherents of different declaratory nuclear strategies of deterrence are predisposed toward defense. The more general question, of whether defense is desirable in any form, and hence what are the prospects for strategic defense, require looking at the entire issue from both strategic and political perspectives as the debate is likely to unfold toward SDI.

Fortunately, it is unnecessary to proceed in a cloud of virtually complete speculation. SDI is, after all, only the latest manifestation of the BMD question, and there is a history of consideration of the strategic defense. The first major evidence of public concern came in the 1960s in the form of the ABM debate, and the substance and outcomes of that debate are instructive in creating some of the boundaries around the ongoing debate. That debate, subsequent thinking and writing on ballistic missile defense, and some newer phenomena not evident at the time help frame how the debate is likely to proceed.

The ABM Debate

The matter of missile defense first came to the public's attention in the early 1960s. The cause was the debates over atmospheric nuclear testing and the test ban. The problem was that although most other nuclear testing programs could accommodate the limitations of underground testing, the embryonic ABM required increasingly unacceptable testing in the atmosphere. According to Freeman Dyson, "The general public was introduced to ABM in the context of the test ban debate, and learned to identify ABM with the unpopular cause of continued atmospheric bomb tests. This was a blow from which ABM never recovered."[1]

ABM was thus a victim of the Limited Test Ban Treaty, but its adherents showed a remarkable resiliency (which has been one of their primary characteristics). Before the end of the decade, various missile defenses schemes were proposed and debated in both the Johnson and Nixon administrations. Ultimately, the result of these debates was to defeat ABM. Assuming that some or all of the SDI technologies reach fruition, there is likely to be yet another debate of the same nature. The question is whether the outcomes of the first debate will help frame the agenda and outcomes of the second.

Let us look back analytically rather than strictly chronologically at the period between about 1967 and 1969, when debate raged in Congress and among the public. Three related factors coalesced to ensure the defeat of ABM: uncertainty over whether ABM would work, reluctance to bear the considerable expense attached to the defense, and objections that ABM would destabilize the nuclear balance. The expert community (especially its scientific segment) largely created the first issue. Just as there is substantial disagreement among physicists and other physical scientists today over whether the SDI technologies will ever mature, there were clearly such disagreements during the 1960s debate as well. The hearings of various congressional committees and subcommittees were well stocked with testimony from one group of reputable and distinguished scientists gravely intoning that ABM was a miraculous technology that would function sensationally, followed by testimony from an equally distinguished group willing to opine with equal vigor that ABM was a hopeless boondoggle that would never produce even a modicum of defense.

The impression that the public and its representatives were clearly left with was one of confusion; if the experts could not agree about ABM, how could the lay public? When this disagreement was placed alongside the general disrepute of ABM from the test ban period and public suspicions captured in John Kennedy's bullet analogy, the public predisposition was not favorable to ABM.

The second and related factor was cost. The price tag placed on Richard Nixon's Sentinel "thin" ABM system was what now seems a modest $5 billion or so, but it seemed like a lot then, particularly in the context of the times.

There were at least two economic factors running specifically against ABM. First, ABM was being proposed directly on the heels of a very expensive offensive force modernization program. To exacerbate the problem, one of the major justifications for ABM was that it was needed to protect those brand new ICBMs, which were deemed vulnerable to Soviet preemptive attack without them. (The Air Force had neglected to mention that vulnerability when proposing Minuteman in the first place.) Many wondered if enough had not already been spent on strategic nuclear weaponry.

The second economic factor was the ongoing war in Vietnam, which was being conducted while President Johnson remained wedded to the expensive series of welfare and entitlement programs known cumulatively as the Great Society. Since he had also elected not to raise taxes to defray the costs of the war, one way to stop the flow of red ink was by economizing on other defense concerns. ABM was a prime candidate for such cutbacks.

These first two factors interacted. ABM was clearly an expensive proposition, but it might have been a tolerable economic sacrifice if there had been general agreement that it was a good investment. The climate of technical uncertainty that surrounded the debate, however, raised the significant prospect that money spent on ABM might be money wasted: ABM looked like an expensive pig in the poke.

The third factor—a theoretical one—was raised in the first chapter. The period of the ABM debate coincided with the most widespread acceptance of the theory of assured destruction. Adherents of assured destruction were prominent in and outside government, and they were reasonably uniform in their opposition to ABM as destabilizing, because it potentially appeared to reduce inhibitions to begin nuclear war.

These factors are helpful in judging the emerging debate over the SDI. Although assured destruction no longer occupies the intellectual high ground that it commanded in the 1960s and thus can probably be dismissed as a debilitating factor, both uncertainty over performance and cost are almost certain to be considerable factors again.

Given the very early stages of development of the SDI technologies, it is not surprising that scientists of great stature are in disagreement about how their investigations will eventually turn out and whether the military potentials will be realized. For advocates, a full-scale debate over those potentials would appear premature and potentially disastrous, since the same lack of consensus evident in the earlier debate would doubtless be evident today.

The same is true of the economic side of the ledger. Depending on whose figures one accepts (as discussed shortly), SDI could be very expensive. Moreover, there are economic parallels with the 1960s.

Two parallels stand out. The first is that the 1983 proposal to develop strategic defenses followed by only about one and a half years the president's announced intention to engage in major offensive force modernization. The situation is not perfectly analogous, of course, because not all the modernization has occurred (and in some specific instances, it may never take place). Nonetheless, the American taxpayers are being asked to digest a double dose of strategic offense and defense in the 1980s, just as they were in the 1960s. Their willingness to do so may be questionable this time, as it was two decades ago.

The second parallel is the budgetary competiton between strategic defense and other national priorities. One of the factors that helped doom ABM was its need to compete for scarce budgetary resources with the Vietnam war. A parallel may currently exist between the SDI and large budget deficits. This parallel and the attending difficulties it might produce could be especially severe if the costs of SDI prove to be quite high, as they may be. Should the decision to fund SDI have a marked impact on deficit sizes, there will be some clear pressures either to sacrifice SDI or to make cuts elsewhere in defense.

The 1980s and beyond, when decisions regarding the SDI will have to be made, are not identical to the 1960s when ABM was defeated. The point of the preceding discussion, of course, is that some rough parallels do exist and could help frame the debate over SDI. The shape of that debate, however, can best be seen by looking at the major arguments that are likely to be put forward both in favor and in opposition to the proposal.

The Case for Strategic Defense

Those who support a movement toward active defenses against ballistic missiles make a number of arguments in support of their advocacy. Different proponents, of course, cite or emphasize different bases of advocacy, but it is possible to array the strongest arguments around five related points. These arguments range from technical feasibility to the imperatives for defense against nuclear winter.

Technical Feasibility

The first argument in support of active defenses is that active defenses against attack are now possible given developments since the ABM debate two decades ago. This assertion, of course, directly contradicts arguments against missile defense that maintain it could never perform adequately, which formed one of the most telling criticisms in the 1960s.

Part of the assertion of technical feasibility is that Kennedy's bullet analogy is misleading and that conceptually, at least, the problem is a great deal simpler than the analogy suggests. Rather, leading proponents Daniel Graham and Gregory Fossedal argue the conceptual simplicity of the problem: "A missile launched at the U.S. travels so fast that if you tossed an ice cube at it and hit it, you would divert it sufficiently to render it impotent. . . . [A] missile's high speed make[s] it vulnerable."[2] The ice cube analogy may, of course, be as misleading as the bullet analogy, since it is no mean task to find a projectile traveling at thousands of miles per hour and then to throw the ice cube accurately enough to strike the projectile. At the same time, the conceptual problems associated with missile defense have always been a good bit simpler than the operational difficulties of designing a missile defense system to actualize the concept.

In essence, there are three operational problems that must be solved for a BMD system to be workable. The first problem is acquisition and tracking. This is essentially a radar problem that is assigned to satellites hovering above the Soviet Union. The second problem is trajectory determination, extrapolating where a projectile will be at a future point in time based on observing it in flight. Given the speeds and short times involved, this is primarily a computing problem. Finally, there is the problem of interception, getting the BMD device to an appropriate point to intercept and destroy or disable the offensive weapon.

Proponents of BMD argue that all these operational problems, each of which represented a major barrier to ABM in the 1960s, either is or soon will be solved. Target acquisition and tracking capabilities have been greatly enhanced by advances in space-based satellite radar capacity, especially in geosynchronous satellites beyond the range of Soviet antisatellite (ASAT) capability. Problems associated with trajectory determination historically were the result of comparatively slow computing times by older generations of computers. Current and future generations presumably are capable of processing data in an adequately timely manner to allow interception, the third problem.

Interceptor improvements have or will soon occur both in "conventional" ABM technology and DET weaponry. In regard to ABMs, the major advancements have been the results of improved microprocessing capabilities. In effect these advances mean that current and future generation ABM interceptors will be equipped with minicomputer guidance systems that will make them more agile (able to respond to evasive actions by the offensive system) and more selective (able to discriminate more effectively between real RVs and chaff decoys). These same kinds of advances in computing efficiency will, presumably, enhance the effectiveness of DET systems by endowing them with the capacity for dealing with a very large and complex attack, such as an all-out Soviet launch.

These sorts of alleged technical capabilities lead proponents to conclude that practical defenses are not somewhere in the faraway future. The relatively recent successful testing of an ABM device over the Pacific range is seen as evidence of this progress. Clarence A. Robinson, Jr., *Aviation Week and Space Technology*'s resident expert in the field, has suggested, on the basis of extrapolation from the *Defensive Technologies Study,* that many of the practical problems associated with space-based systems are well on their way to solution as well.[3]

The ultimate form of the defense in these advocacies is the so-called layered defense. In this scheme, the BMD system would consist of both traditional ABMs and DET systems.[4] In a commonly discussed form, rising Soviet missiles would first be attacked in boost phase by space-based laser systems. Those rockets that survived would then be attacked in intermediary flight by exoatmospheric ABMs with powerful warheads of their own. What little of the attacking force survived these onslaughts would then be attacked by endoatmospheric ABM interceptors and ground-based directed energy weapons such as neutral charged-particle beams. This combination, according to the proponents, could produce the leakproof defense that critics argue is unattainable. Moreover, the proponents say, this kind of system could be erected in stages as the various technologies become available.

Reinforcing Deterrence
The second and third arguments are related to one another in two ways. First, both represent rejections of the assured destruction logic that was used with great effect during the ABM debate. Second, they share the contention that missile defenses are stabilizing rather than destabilizing, both in terms of deterrence and crisis (thus deterrence) stability sequentially.

The second argument is that missile defenses can reinforce rather than detract from deterrence, especially if the erection of those defenses is accompanied by substantial reductions in offensive arms. The point here, congruent with the various interpretations of what deters, is to maintain the situation where both sides continue to believe that a nuclear exchange between them cannot be successful. As long as that situation adheres, the deterrence system remains stable. As Herman Kahn puts it, "One significant indication of the effectiveness of deterrence is that the Soviet Union and the United States share the belief that a nuclear war would only begin out of desperation or inadvertence."[5]

Ruling out volition as the proximate cause of nuclear hostilities, the question is how one can best maintain the assessment of the consequences that produce the inhibition. Part of the answer can be missile defenses, which can reinforce either side's uncertainty about their ability to gain from initiating war. As Keith Payne and Colin S. Gray put it, "Even . . . limited conventional defensive coverage for U.S. retaliatory forces would create enormous uncertainties for Soviet planners considering the effectiveness of a strategic first strike."[6]

Graham and Fossedal, in typically expansive style, concur on the inhibiting effect that these uncertainties could produce: "Would a defense be adequate if it provided no rock-bottom guarantees at all—but did throw so much uncertainty into the calculations of someone contemplating an attack on the U.S. that they would decide not to?"[7] Since their book is an open polemic for the defense, they of course answer the question affirmatively. These advocacies that suggest a limited defense is stabilizing stop far short of the president's stated hope that missile defenses can become so effective as to render offensive nucleartipped ballistic missiles obsolete.

There is not universal concurrence on this point. Among other things, those who make the case that a residually effective defensive system is better than none have always faced the substantial criticism that arsenal sizes are currently so great that they would make no practical difference. On the one hand, even if only a relatively small percentage of offensive missiles (say, in extremis, several hundred) penetrated to target, the result would still be devastation on a scale unprecedented in human history. On the other hand, offensive arsenals are so large and diverse that they could easily overwhelm any defense that might be arrayed against them, making the defense impossible.

This criticism is recognized at official levels. Reacting to it, Secretary of Defense Weinberger presaged the New Strategic Concept by arguing the synergism between defensive build-up and offensive build-down. "For the longer term, offensive force reductions and defensive technologies can be mutually reinforcing. Effective defenses that reduce the utility of ballistic missiles and other offensive forces have the potential for increasing the likelihood of negotiated reductions of those offensive forces."[8] This general notion has begun attracting attention. Recently, it has been at the core of the early Reagan approach to the Geneva arms talks, linking the START/

SALT-like negotiations on offensive arms to the SDI in the form of the New Strategic Concept. Alvin Weinberg and Jack Barkenbus call this basic approach the defense-protected build-down. Graham and Fossedal add that it would reinforce their strategy of "assured survival" under which "we can reasonably project that strategic defense would be more likely to prevent all-out war—with the added, crucial advantage that if it does not, we are not totally without defense."[10] We will examine this argument in more detail in the concluding chapter.

Increased Stability

The third and related argument, also in contradiction to "traditional" assured destruction thought, is that missile defenses reinforce the stability of the deterrence system, especially at time of crisis. The basis of this assertion is the contention that missile defenses are nonprovocative weapons. By this the proponents mean that defensive weapons cannot be used offensively to attack enemy offensive forces preemptively, so that they do not contribute to a decision that it is necessary to launch first to avoid destruction of those forces.

If one accepts this contention, then missile defenses have at least two salutary effects. First, they are crisis-stabilizing because they cannot be employed preemptively. As a result, one adversary or the other facing a defensive system is not drawn into a "use them or lose them" mode that could grease the slippery slide to nuclear war initiation even more. Instead, to the degree that the systems are effective, the result is to render the offensive forces impotent, so that their use preemptively is pointless. Second, to the degree that the defense is used to protect retaliatory forces successfully, they reinforce the viability of maintaining a retaliatory strategy and present the potential aggressor with the prospect of effective retaliation.

This basic distinction may be a bit too facile, particularly regarding the potentials of technologies included in the SDI. While it is true that most of the applied research currently underway projects, say, space-based lasers in a defensive role, the creation of adequately powerful lasers might make them dually capable—usable in both offensive and defensive modes. What if, for instance, a space-based laser could be devised that could attack Soviet missiles in their silos (for instance by melting the covers shut) rather than waiting for them to be fired. Would such an attack, or even its contemplation, be considered offensive or defensive? It might be considered simple offensive-damage limitation (an arguable form of very active defense) by the weapon possessor, but would almost certainly be viewed as an offensive weapon by the side at which it was aimed.

Moral Concerns

The fourth argument is moral and ethical in nature. One of the anomalies of assured destruction theory is the horrible nature of the threat it makes toward the Soviet Union should it attack the United States. In essence, the threat is genocidal, for it involves randomly killing some arbitrarily determined proportion of the Soviet population as vengeance for an act almost all of them had nothing to do with personally. It recalls the German reprisal against the Czechs at Lidice during World War II on a very large scale, and as such is a morally reprehensible threat to carry out (and possibly to make). Another anomaly is that the whole threat system relies on a self-enforced abstention from any attempt at self-defense, since such actions could loosen inhibitions. Since a major traditional purpose of military force is to protect national territory and the lives of the citizens, this strategy creates ethical difficulties for the military.

There is not, of course, universal agreement that assured destruction is a moral indefensible position. Those who defend the concept argue that the only true morality in the nuclear age is deterrence, given the consequences of its failure. From this position, they further maintain that assured destruction, because it describes what a nuclear war in fact would look like and because its threat is maximally horrifying and thus deterring, best reinforces deterrence and hence is the most morally lofty position to take.

Those who feel assured destruction is morally bankrupt and who also favor the defense argue in response that deterrence can in fact fail, despite our efforts to avoid it. Should that awful event transpire and the assured destruction threat have to be carried out, it would be a moral atrocity of outrageous proportions. Moreover, the fact that adherence to the doctrine had prevented any attempt at self-defense would prove to be ethically unconscionable. As

Payne and Gray argue, "The central problem of nuclear deterrence is that no offensive deterrent, no matter how fearsome, is likely to work forever, and the consequences of its failure would be intolerable for civilization."[11] Making specific reference to the contribution that space-based lasers (SBL) could make to solving this dilemma, analyst Barry Smernoff adds that "the emergency of SBL technology creates a new alternative for coping with the seemingly inscrutable problems and ethical dilemmas of nuclear war and nuclear weapons."[12] It is this kind of moral argument that underpins a good deal of the president's advocacy of the SDI technologies.

Nuclear Winter
The fifth argument is of recent vintage and is, in fact, a position just beginning to take shape. It arises from a problem called the "nuclear winter" and presented to the strategic community by a group of physicists.[13] Briefly put, this phenomenon refers to the climatological and biological consequences of the detonation of a large number of nuclear weapons, presumably by the United States and the Soviet Union. Such an exchange, especially if directed against urban population concentrations, would create enormous firestorms as the cities burned. Those firestorms in turn would inject tremendous quantities of soot and other particulants into the upper atmosphere which would gradually create a cloud cover girdling the globe and effectively blocking out the warmth of the sun's rays. This would lower the Earth's surface temperature by up to an average of 20 degrees Fahrenheit for up to a year. Crops would be killed, large amounts of surface water would freeze, and the result would be large-scale starvation and freezing to add to the list of nuclear war's deadly effects. Civilization as we know it could effectively end before the winter's effects ceased.[14]

There is general, if not universal, agreement that at some level of exchange that is as yet unspecified and possibly unspecifiable, the winter phenomenon would ensue. Both Americans and Soviet scientists are continuing to study the problem; at this point, the Soviets seem even more pessimistic about the effects than the Americans. What is not so clear are the policy implications of this phenomenon.

Responses at the policy level are only beginning to emerge and have to date been somewhat disappointing. Mostly, analysts have used nuclear winter as a way to reinforce whatever deterrence theology they already supported. Thus, the disarmers use the winter as proof of the need to rid the world of nuclear weapons, assured destruction adherents say that this simply specifies the disaster more fully, and supporters of limited nuclear options argue that the winter only makes limitation below the threshold level all the more necessary.

Within the specific debate over missile defense and the SDI, nuclear winter can be used to support a movement to defense, and especially to countervalue defense. The logic of this position is that an urban defense could keep the fury of an attack against combustible targets such as cities at a small enough level as to stay below the threshold for the winter. In essence, ballistic missile defense becomes a hedge against the winter.

This position will doubtless not be universally accepted. For one thing, there are very real uncertainties both about the effectiveness that any defensive system can achieve and about the level which would be adequate to induce the winter. Thus, a defense that was designed to defend cities could prove inadequate in the real event, a discovery that we would make as we slipped into the winter's darkness. On the other hand, the hedge created by BMD could prevent that from occurring. Without doubt, the combination of BMD and the nuclear winter provides, at the risk of a pun, great fuel for continuing debate and discussion.

The Case against Strategic Defense

As stated earlier, advocacy of missile defense has historically been somewhat disreputable in the American debate. Whether the reason for this disrepute was the early association of BMD with the unpopular cause of atmospheric testing or nagging skepticism about whether defense against ballistically delivered nuclear munitions was possible, the opponents have historically outnumbered the proponents.

The president's Star Wars advocacy has brought the proponents out of the closet, as it were, and it has also brought the opponents out of their ABM Treaty-induced hibernation. The balance of opinion has shifted from where it was located twenty years ago, but the opponents have reemerged in force. As they mount their case against BMD, three arguments seem likely to be most prominent and potentially effective.

Assured Destruction

The first argument is the traditional assured destruction position against missile defenses. This position, of course, typifies BMD as a destabilizing chimera. The charge of destabilization is based on the notion that BMD undercuts the conditions on which assured destruction, which is used interchangeably with deterrence, rests. It does so by producing the promise of protection against attack, which is destabilizing because useful inhibitions grounded on the certainty of retaliatory vengeance are weakened. BMD makes, or appears to make, the consequences of nuclear war initiation less personally and societally devastating and thus easier to reach. The cruel irony, of course, is that defense would, in the eyes of most adherents of assured destruction, prove illusory, since assured destruction adherents are generally skeptical that such a defense can be mounted successfully.

Destabilization during Transition

This first argument has a familiar ring, having been used extensively during the ABM debate. The second argument, however, is of more recent vintage. This argument speaks to the possible destabilization that would occur during the period of transition from a defenseless world to a world in which the defense played a role. Since neither side has ever fielded meaningful defenses in the past, and since thinking about nuclear weapons on both sides has been dominated by the supremacy of offensive weapons, the problem of "how to get from here to there" is difficult, both in intellectual and mechanical ways.

The intellectual part of the problem is that thinking, planning, and theorizing about strategic weapons has been absolutely dominated by offensive considerations at least since the dawn of the missile age. All our theories underlying declaratory and employment strategies are based on defenselessness against nuclear attack, and we simply have no developed intellectual constructs to encompass strategic defenses into schemes for continued deterrence (a point elaborated in chapter 6). Since the defense is becoming a real possibility, incorporating defensive considerations into the mix is mandatory if we are to avoid a technological surprise—for example, Maneuverable Reentry Vehicle (MaRV) and Stealth technologies for which strategy is unprepared.

The physical aspect of the problem is how to make the transition to a world where defenses are a factor. As a problem, one must consider the possible sources of difficulty and instability that would accompany the transition. The problem is more or less difficult depending on whether Soviet and American deployments are symmetrical or asymmetrical.

The less troublesome possibility is the situation where both sides more or less simultaneously develop and decide to deploy systems of roughly equivalent capability (regardless of the level of effectiveness). In that circumstance, it is possible to use arms control processes to effect an orderly deployment of such systems, so that the changeover would be symmetrical, and neither side would have particular advantage at any point in the process of change. Whether the resulting offensive–defensive mix would add to stability or instability is, of course, largely a matter of beliefs about whether or not BMD is stabilizing.

The more troublesome possibility is where one side or the other makes a substantial breakthrough that would allow it to deploy a system for which the adversary has no counterpart or one that is markedly inferior. A dramatic breakthrough by, for instance, the United States in one of the SDI technologies that the Soviets cannot match would seem to offer the best possibility in this regard. If exploited, such a situation could provide the possessor with great advantage.

The potential source of instability arises from the disadvantaged state realizing its situation will be materially weakened once deployment is completed by the other. If the defenses are as formidable as optimistic appraisals of SDI suggest they could be, the nonpossessor would be left with a largely useless offensive force which could not successfully penetrate to target. The result could be to place the nonpossessor in a "use them or leave them useless" dilemma during the deployment stage. What this means is that the nonpossessor might be tempted to attack before the systems became operational, since it knows that its forces would be impotent once deployment was complete.

Not all observers think this problem is severe. Graham and Fossedal, in particular, dismiss it: "Would the Soviets attack as we complete our . . . defense? Of course not; no fundamental change in the balance of power is threatened. . . . The stronger the U.S. defenses become, the less sense a Soviet strike makes—but the process is marginal, not an all-for-one shot."[15]

High Cost of Active Defense

The final negative argument is the cost of active defenses, an argument of special relevance regarding the SDI. Cost was, after all, one of the major stumbling blocks faced by ABM, when the estimates were a comparatively modest $5 billion or so. Depending on the source one consults and the kind of system one envisages, the kinds of defenses one could deploy now vary enormously from that figure.

As is explained in a later chapter more fully, the basic disagreement about SDI costs revolves around the number of satellites which would be necessary for a space-based defense. The individual satellites would cost several billion dollars apiece; low estimates tend to assume a relatively modest deployment, while larger estimates assume more satellites will be needed.

Cost estimates also vary significantly depending on the kind of defense that is envisaged. At the low end of the spectrum are advocates of the high frontier, who advocate deploying so-called readily available technology and who maintain that such a system could be effective at or around $12 billion.[16]

Other observers (especially those looking at systems employing SDI components) are less sanguine about the modesty of cost involved. Depending upon satellite numbers needed (about which only guesses can be made at this point), costs vary wildly. As one observer catalogues, "Estimates of the amount needed to make the new system operational and effective range from $10 billion to $500 billion."[17] That estimate was made in 1982; a more recent guess based on a comprehensive system ups the ante: "The goal . . . is to have a multilayered ballistic missile defense in place within 20 years at a cost estimated at between $250–500 billion."[18] Those kinds of figures will produce public and congressional opposition, and that opposition will be buttressed by two bedeviling factors. The first is that the proponents will not, with any exactitude, be able to demonstrate that what they propose will work with the kind of precision that would justify the expenditure. In a manner reminiscent of the ABM debate, there will undoubtedly be disagreement in the expert community that will leave the public and its representatives wondering if they are being asked to buy a pig in the poke once again.

The second bedeviling factor is the possibility that the expense will be open-ended, producing an arms race in space where BMD satellites invite the deployment of ASAT satellites, redundancy in systems deployments, and the like. Beyond fully militarizing the last frontier, the competition could be extremely expensive and long term, meaning that even very high cost estimates could represent only the tip of the iceberg.

Conclusion

The purpose of this chapter has been to lay out, in a general way, some of the major bases on which advocacy and opposition to SDI are likely to occur during the developing debate over strategic defenses. As the discussion is intended to show, the arguments on both sides are strong but not overwhelming, so that the outcome is not predetermined.

Implicit in the discussions in support of SDI and defense generally are the dual assumptions that the defense is both possible and desirable. At least with regard to SDI, the truth of the assumption about practicability is unknown at this point and could be answered negatively or positively in the long run. If a negative response is what science and engineering ultimately offer, then the entire debate about desirability is moot. That latter debate, as has been argued, has a slightly theological air about it.

Other questions remain that are of a more technical and doctrinal nature, and the answers that one derives to those kinds of concerns have a strong impact on whether or not the ultimate judgment about SDI should be positive or negative. The discussion in the next four chapters centers on these important issues, following which some conclusions will be derived in the final chapter.

Notes

1. Freeman Dyson, *Weapons and Hope* (New York: Harper & Row, 1984), p. 74.
2. Daniel O. Graham and Gregory A. Fossedal, *A Defense that Defends: Blocking Nuclear Attack* (Old Greenwich, Conn.: Devin–Adair Publishers, 1983), p. 44.
3. See, for instance, "Study Urges Exploiting of Technologies," *Aviation Week and Space Tecnology* 119 (September/October 1983):50–51; and "Panel Urges Boost-Phase Intercept," *Aviation Week and Space Technology* 119 (December 1983):50–61.
4. This approach is discussed in some detail in Donald M. Snow, *The Nuclear Future: Toward a Strategy of Uncertainty* (Tuscaloosa, Ala.: University of Alabama Press, 1983), chap. 3.
5. This point is made strongly by the late Herman Kahn in his posthumously released book *Thinking about the Unthinkable in the 1980s* (New York Simon and Schuster, 1984), p. 37.
6. Keith Payne and Colin S. Gray, "Nuclear Policy and the Defensive Transition," *Foreign Affairs* 62, no. 4 (Spring 1984):824.
7. Graham and Fossedal, *A Defense that Defends*, p. 45.
8. Caspar Weinberger, *Annual Report to the Congress, Fiscal Year 1985* (Washington, D.C.: Government Printing Office, February 1, 1984), p. 58.
9. Alvin M. Weinberg and Jack N. Barkenbus, "Stabilizing Star Wars," *Foreign Policy* 54 (Spring 1984):164.
10. Graham and Fossedal, *A Defense that Defends*, p. 113.
11. Payne and Gray, "Nuclear Policy," p. 820.
12. Barry J. Smernoff, "The Strategic Value of Space-Based Laser Weapons," *Air University Review* 33, no. 5 (March/April 1982):14.
13. Carl Sagan, "Nuclear War and the Climatic Catastrophe," *Foreign Affairs* 62, no. 2 (Winter 1983/1984):257–92.
14. For a recent introduction, see Paul Ehrlich, Carl Sagan, Donald Kennedy, and Walter Orr Roberts, *The Cold and the Dark: The World after Nuclear War* (New York: W.W. Norton, 1984).
15. Graham and Fossedal, *A Defense that Defends*, p. 120.
16. *Ibid.*, p.55.
17. Steven E. Cady, "Beam Weapons in Space: A Reality We Must Confront," *Air University Review*, 33, no. 4 (May/June 1982):37.
18. William E. Burrows, "Ballistic Missile Defense: The Illusion of Security," *Foreign Affairs*, 62, no. 4 (Spring 1984): p. 843.

3
Demonstrating Strategic Defense
The Burdens of Proof

If such a weapons system can be devised, it would be an incentive to
the Soviets to reduce or eliminate missiles, since we've *proven* that it's
possible to be invulnerable to an attack.
President Reagan, election day interview, November 5, 1984
(Emphasis added)

E ver since its unveiling, the question of feasibility has shaped
judgments on and even the presentation of President Ronald
Reagan's Strategic Defense Initiative. Reagan's own announcement
of the program recognized that "eliminating the threat posed by
strategic nuclear missiles" would be "a formidable technical task
. . . that may not be accomplished before the end of this century."

Since the president's speech, administration officials have con-
tinually been confronted with the questions "Can it work?" and,
just as important, "How can we know?" The president's aides have
usually responded by stressing that the SDI is a research program
and not a decision to deploy weapons. The question of deploying
an actual strategic defense system, they have emphasized, would
arise only if and when the SDI research generated options for effective defenses that were achievable and affordable.

Great uncertainty exists despite this apparently prudent position. Partly to blame, no doubt, are the administration's constantly
shifting rationales for the program, which make it impossible to
know how the SDI will affect future United States strategic planning. United States officials variously have predicted that the SDI

Portions of this chapter are adapted with permission from Gary Guertner, "What is
'Proof'?" *Foreign Policy* 59 (Summer 1985): 73–84. Copyright 1985 by the Carnegie
Endowment for International Peace.

will replace deterrence, enhance deterrence, or defend retaliatory forces or possibly America's population. Congress has been told that strategic defense is not an optional program, but is central to American military planning, as well as that SDI is simply a research program to see what develops.

The administration refined its position when preparations for the 1985 round of the Geneva arms control negotiations prompted general coupling of SDI and long-range negotiating strategy. The general call for a research program became the basis for a new strategic concept presented by Secretary of State Shultz to former Soviet Foreign Minister Gromyko during the January 1985 meeting that brought both sides back to the arms control negotiating table. The new concept, reportedly developed by Paul Nitze, calls for "radical reductions" in offensive weapons over the next ten years, and for a period of mutual transition to effective nonnuclear defense forces as technology makes such options available.[1]

To its credit, the performance criteria the administration has developed in its promotion and defense of the SDI have been demanding. Emerging technologies must produce defensive systems that are:

1. Technologically achievable and reliable against Soviet offensive forces,
2. Effective (lethal),
3. Survivable,
4. Affordable in terms of total systems costs,
5. Cost-effective at the margin (An increment of defense is cheaper to deploy than an increment of offensive countermeasures.),[2]
6. Capable of enhancing deterrence and strategic stability.[3]

The uncertainty surrounding SDI's technical feasibility and cost-effectiveness, however, will persist for a more fundamental reason. Many of the answers to SDI critics and skeptics can be learned only by the kind of field testing barred by the Anti-Ballistic Missile Treaty of 1972 or by actual use during a nuclear war. If Congress authorizes all or most of the $26 billion the administration has planned through FY 1989, a great deal will undoubtedly be learned about promising new technologies that new American strategic concepts will require. But not even the most ambitiously funded research program will be able to provide the information needed to make a scientifically informed decision about strategic defense. Without understanding the ambiguities and controversies that will still remain, Congress and the public may succumb to a misplaced confidence that SDI research alone can illuminate a risk-free path to a safer, defense-dominated world. In the process, an idea capable of destabilizing today's nuclear balance may pass the point of no return, riding only bureaucratic momentum and the technically groundless optimism of vested political and professional interests.

Risks from SDI research, even in its current embryonic and seemingly innocent forms, can already be identified. In a speech before the National Academy of Sciences, Gerald Yonas, senior scientist at the Strategic Defense Initiative Organization, described his office's mission as a search for the limits of technology, for the vulnerability of systems to countermeasures, and for cost-effectiveness. Measured by these criteria, the least promising technologies will be winnowed out. Winnowing out is the most that should be expected from SDIO scientists and engineers. The history of project officers becoming attached to systems to which they have devoted time, money, prestige, and perhaps future careers is a source of legitimate concern. Strong political commitment and technological ambiguity have worked in the past to sustain programs, even through periods of strong opposition and flawed performance. No matter how many approaches are winnowed out, these nonscientific factors may fuel faith that an answer lies just around the corner.

Further, overt political pressures can easily distort technological objectivity when the time comes to make that "informed" decision to deploy. Even if objectivity survives the political process, the political community may be too innocent of technical details and the uncertainties in "scientific" methods to evaluate innovations properly. Similarly, the technologically competent may be equally unaware of military considerations and unable to evaluate the impact of technology on war and strategy.

These problems will usually be exacerbated by the dynamics of bureaucratic decision making. The scientists and engineers in SDIO, in the Pentagon's Defense Advanced Research Projects Agency

(DARPA), and in the defense industry will almost certainly produce a system that generates major controversies, even from within. If there were a consensus within the scientific community, wise political leadership could reasonably defer. But when reputable scientists are divided, as they are likely to be, what will politicians do? They are likely to base their decisions on political preference rather than on scientific proof.

The primacy of politics over science is already apparent in the optimistic administration statements about the status of emerging technologies required for a layered defense. In a January 1985 White House booklet entitled *The President's Strategic Defense Initiative,* for example, the president states that "new technologies are now at hand which may make possible a truly effective non-nuclear defense." The SDIO, in fact, spent most of 1985 evaluating what its director, General James Abrahamson, describes as "horse race contracts."[4] These contracts were awarded in a competition for the best—and most quickly produced—concept of mission and its required technical capabilities. References in public speeches to "horse race contracts" and "architectural design concepts" mean that SDI is still in its formative stage. No one can predict what may result from this contractual laying of track on which the appropriations train may roll for the next two decades or more.

Most scientists agree that many individual components of strategic defense can be developed. Individual weapons could be tested and deployed in space or on the Earth's surface. Battle management satellites, radar, and millions of lines of computer instructions could be integrated into a real-time intelligence system to acquire and track a nuclear warhead from launch to destruction. The problem, however, is that during the testing phases of SDI, the success of individual components will not prove the reliability of the entire system. In the real world, the transition from offensive systems which have dominated strategic nuclear deterrence to a new strategic concept based on defense will be filled with considerable uncertainty.

The possibility of gaining a meaningful understanding of how defensive systems would operate in a wartime environment, for example, is almost nil, because of the fundamental difference between testing offensive and defensive weapons. Relatively reliable predictions of offensive-force performance can be gleaned from limited tests of individual weapons and components. Successfully firing individual intercontinental ballistic missiles and submarine-launched ballistic missiles down a long test range can give offensive planners confidence that a high percentage of deployed systems would reach their targets during wartime.[5]

The performance of defensive systems, however, consists of much more than launching essentially identical individual weapons according to a particular targeting plan. Instead, defensive systems are integrated units that must be able to intercept large numbers of simultaneously launched weapons before they reach their targets. Full-scale tests against some five- to ten-thousand weapons are obviously impossible. Thus, because defense planners see only isolated pieces, they cannot discern the entire puzzle. Claims of systematic effectiveness will never be entirely demonstrable, since only a full-scale attack could demonstrate the reliability of sensors, communications, and weapons operating together in the most complex battle management system ever devised.

Even if all these questions could be answered, the answers might never take root. The problems associated with strategic defense are not static obstacles that can be leaped or sidestepped. Instead, they are created by an adversary who is actively trying to overwhelm, circumvent, or in some way negate U.S. efforts over time. It is misleading to talk about low costs or favorable cost-exchange ratios between defense and offense as if there will be a time and a clearly delineated posture that, once reached, will permit the defense to declare final victory. We are not dealing just with a technical system, but with a strategy for defending the United States against a nuclear attack. As chapter 5 illustrates, strategy requires many systems, all of which may be challenged by countervailing Soviet strategy and technology.

The primary effect of competition based on so much uncertainty is to push both sides toward worst-case judgments about the effectiveness of its own and its adversary's defensive systems. The same logic which drives one to doubt one's own capabilities drives one to expect the enemy to be effective. In order to remedy perceived shortcomings and reduce uncertainties, both sides are likely to undertake defensive and offensive improvements that could only prompt similar, redoubled efforts by the other side. These uncertainties combine to create a strategic environment in which crude estimates replace tangible evidence as building blocks of perceived reality.

Such uncertainty could complicate offensive and defensive arms control efforts by clouding judgments of what systems could be limited or foreclosed without jeopardizing national security. Offensive forces, for example, could be expanded by the side perceiving inferiority in defensive capability. Either side could seek countervailing advantages in offense or defense. Thus, the competition could gain momentum not only through technological opportunism, but also from the fear of falling behind.

Legal Obstacles to Demonstrating Defenses

SDI supporters should not forget the importance of maintaining the existing arms control regime and of preserving the negotiating process aimed at reducing offensive arms levels. The Defensive Technologies Study Team, which examined the SDI's feasibility for the Pentagon, not only emphasized that the cost and technological complexity of strategic defenses would be open-ended without arms control agreements, but also stressed that interim deployments of ballistic missile defenses, specifically "point defenses" designed to protect missile silos, would be cost-effective only against "constrained threats." The policy quandary sure to arise in the future will result from the panel's recommendation to pursue a vigorous research and development program and to demonstrate "intermediate technologies." Demonstrations are essential to proving the systems potential, but little can be done within the limits of the ABM Treaty—in other words, without destroying treaty constraints that the panel has identified as essential for establishing cost and technological boundaries to the development of strategic defense.

Article V of the ABM Treaty forbids the parties to "develop," "test," or "deploy" sea-based, air-based, space-based, or mobile land-based ABM systems or components. By failing specifically to proscribe it, the treaty tacitly permits some activity that could be called research. But the line between prohibited "development" and permitted "research" is vague and subject to conflicting interpretations. Growing SDI research budgets will inevitably build pressures and create constituencies to assault that line either directly or under cover of treaty ambiguities.

During treaty ratification hearings, Gerard Smith, former director of the Arms Control and Disarmament Agency (ACDA) and negotiator of the ABM Treaty, told the Senate Committee on Armed Services that:

> The SALT negotiating history clearly supports the following interpretation. The obligation not to develop such systems, devices or warheads would be applicable only to that stage of development which follows laboratory development and testing. The prohibitions on development contained in the ABM Treaty would start at that part of the development process where field testing is initiated on either a prototype or breadboard model. It was understood by both sides that the prohibition on "development" applies to activities involved after a component moves from the laboratory development and testing stage to the field testing stage wherever performed. The fact that early stages of the development process, such as laboratory testing, would pose problems for verification by national technical means is an important consideration in reaching this definition. Exchanges with the Soviet Delegation made clear that this definition is also the Soviet interpretation of the term "development."[6]

Ambassador Smith's statement meant that the "development" stage is only reached when a prototype begins undergoing field testing. Field testing is the dividing line because development and testing in the laboratory would be difficult to verify. Smith's definition (which received no serious challenge at the time) linked development to activities that can be observed by national technical means (intelligence means to monitor treaty compliance), even if such activities do not reach the level of full-scale testing. Laboratory development and testing, even of prototypes, constitute research and are not prohibited.

The Soviet definition of prohibited development is equally flexible. Former defense minister A. A. Grechko, speaking at the session of the Supreme Soviet Presidium ratifying the ABM Treaty stated:

> The treaty on limiting ABM systems provides for a quantitatively small development of ABM facilities by the USSR and the United

States, and prohibits the handover of these facilities to other states or the deployment of them outside the countries' national territories. At the same time it imposes no limitations on the performance of research and experimental work aimed at resolving the problem of defending the country against nuclear missile attack.[7]

Both sides agree on the importance of maintaining research programs to provide each with *insurance* against sudden advantages by the opponent and *incentives* for complying with current and future treaties. But new defensive technologies such as lasers, particle beams, sensors, and kinetic energy weapons spark new controversies over article V prohibitions and the extent to which they should apply to activities inside the laboratory. Both sides have approached this point in their current research programs. Like runners anticipating the starting gun, they seem poised to begin the race if and when treaty obstacles are removed.

Lawyers from the Department of Defense, the State Department, and the Arms Control and Disarmament Agency determine whether SDI activities comply with the ABM Treaty. Like other lawyers, however, they do not base their advice on some objective standard. They are not judges; they represent their organizations' positions within the interagency process. Legal analysis, therefore, is the captive of the same interagency conflicts that paralyzed nearly all other arms control issues during the first Reagan administration.

Although avoiding further erosion of the ABM Treaty has been a declared goal in both capitals, current research programs increase the likelihood that Washington will attempt to negotiate treaty modifications that would permit more extensive testing of SDI technologies. General Abrahamson has already anticipated the political pressures against current treaty constraints. In a speech before the American Institute of Aeronautics and Astronautics, he argued:

> As we take aboard larger budgets, we must demonstrate that we are responsible stewards. . . . There is no way, even if Congress believes in the idea, that it will continue to put out multiple billion dollar budgets if the technologies can't be demonstrated.[8]

Pressure from administration officials and from a pro-administration faction in Congress to demonstrate the existence of real rather than theoretical bargaining chips has collided with the desire to maintain existing arms control agreements. Early evidence of this could be seen in Congress's reaction to SDI proponents who attempted to open a wedge in the administration's original interpretation of "Agreed Statement D" to the ABM Treaty, which permits research, development, and testing of ABM systems "based on other physical properties" such as lasers or particle beams. Treaty supporters argue that "Agreed Statement D" does not allow what article V, the heart of the treaty, prohibits—the development and testing of *any* missile defenses other than fixed, land-based systems. This prohibition includes new systems based on "other physical properties," and it rules out development and testing of space-based systems or components.[9]

The prodevelopment case is legally weak, but may gain momentum because the technical and economic feasibility of the transition to a defense-dominant world cannot be known until technical developments make clear choices of systems possible.

Proving Cost-effectiveness

The warring factions in Congress will be influenced most by SDI costs and by estimates of the cost-exchange ratios between defensive and offensive countermeasures. The complexity of this debate is clear from the widely divergent estimates of the number of satellites required for a credible layered defense. No single issue in the strategic defense debate is more divisive, as table 3–1 indicates.

The great variance in satellite-force size estimates stems from often unstated assumptions concerning such factors as a satellite's orbital time (low-flying satellites can orbit Earth in ninety minutes); the time spent over the target area during a single orbit; destructive payloads; the range of weapons on board; the time required for target acquisition; dwell time (the time required for destruction of an ICBM booster); slew, or retargeting, time; the dispersal of Soviet ballistic missiles; the sequence of launches (mass or phased); warning time; decision time; battle management capabilities; and the reliability of ground-based terminal defenses. It should not be surprising that estimates of satellite constellation size vary so widely at this stage of SDI research.

Table 3–1

Recent Estimates of the Number of Satellites Required for a Credible Layered Defense

Union of Concerned Scientists	300
Office of Technology Assessment	160
Livermore Laboratory	90
Drell, Farley, and Holloway	320
High Frontier	432[a]
Brzezinski, Jastrow, and Kampelman	114

[a]This figure refers to kinetic energy weapons; the other estimates refer to lasers.

Resolution of these differences is essential to the future of SDI, since satellite battle stations could cost as much as an aircraft carrier but would have a considerably shorter operational life. The methodological battle over calculations of these numbers remains intense, and debate will not be closed easily, since satellite numbers must be responsive to unknown Soviet countermeasures. Prudent planners must apply the same technological optimism to countermeasures that they apply to emerging SDI technologies. Judgments of a system's costs and complexity, therefore, cannot be reached through estimates of its effectiveness against a static level of Soviet forces—currently, fourteen hundred ICBMs.

A realistic estimate of the cost of strategic defense should include the costs of defending the system or making it survivable; of maintaining and replacing over time satellite battle stations and supporting command, communication, and control systems; of devising defenses against bombers and cruise missiles as well as ballistic missiles; and of larger conventional forces. In addition, clear limits on the growth of Soviet offensive forces must be established and codified by treaty.

Achieving these criteria will at best be difficult and may prove impossible. Many are being ignored entirely by supporters of strategic defense who, like physicists Robert Jastrow and Gregory Canavan, have made optimistic estimates of satellite-force size and, therefore, of total acquisition costs. Once deployments have begun, however, today's optimists will likely revert to their more traditional tendency to issue worst-case assessments of Soviet capabilities to justify more resources for an ever-expanding program that includes offensive-force modernization.

Certainly the United States could not risk neglecting its offensive forces in the face of massive expansion and improvement of Soviet offensive forces to counter ballistic missile defenses. American technology may be quite capable of countering those countermeasures, but only at correspondingly increased systems complexity and cost. And even these defensive counters will represent just one more step in the ongoing contest between offense and defense. It may be instructive to recall the estimates that were made early in the Manhattan Project. As difficult as developing the first atom bomb was, the initial cost estimate were only $100 million in 1942 dollars. Actual costs turned out to be $2 billion—and there were no Japanese countermeasures.[10]

When confronting a powerful adversary rather than a nearly prostrate enemy, however, methodological and perceptual factors in cost calculations must be employed even more carefully. For example, offensive and defensive costs do not increase linearly. For the Soviets, unit costs of offensive weapons may go down as they use their large, well established infrastructure and hot ICBM production lines to turn out more missiles. By contrast, United States defensive systems are still in their research stage. Continuing research, development, testing, and production costs will probably exceed the unit costs of Soviet offensive increases for years to come until an equally solid base has been established in defensive design, performance, and production. Defense may eventually win the cost-exchange competition by achieving lower marginal costs, but only in the long run and with many uncertainties along the way. In short, Soviet per unit offensive costs could decrease while United States defensive expenditures increase rapidly.

Moreover, Moscow can be expected to spend whatever is necessary to maintain the forces required to execute its strategic doctrine, whatever the costs of overwhelming United States defenses. The Soviets will face technical hurdles, but do not face some of the more formidable political obstacles confronted by American planners operating in a highly pluralistic political and economic system that is far more difficult to squeeze and mobilize than its Soviet counterpart. The technical and political hurdles may be offsetting, but the relative burdens and decisions to mobilize resources occur in radically different political cultures.

If Congress could clearly see how high the final price tag may be, strategic defense would probably have little chance of surviving the scrutiny of deficit-minded legislators. But incremental funding, technological optimism, ambiguous standards of proof (for example, validation of components rather than systems reliability), and predictably shrill Soviet reactions may combine to propel it through the appropriations process for many years. This process may resemble a recipe the late Senator Everett Dirksen once read during a Senate filibuster. His recipe (read "tactic") for cooking frogs cautioned against plopping them directly into boiling water because they would jump right out and mess up the kitchen. "Its better to put them in a pot of cool water, turn the heat on low, cover the pot, and bring the poor critters to a slow boil." Senator Dirksen would have known how to get appropriations for SDI.

Strategic defense may prove to be the wave of the future, but the scientists and engineers inside and outside government who can lead the way into this unchartered world have an obligation to hold their professions and their work to high standards. Scientific objectivity should rise above partisan political debate. Scientists should speak out when technological ambiguity is exploited to anchor political arguments that misrepresent science. Vast sums of money, a wall of secrecy that limits peer review, and strong political commitment for deployment are not the ideal ingredients for "proving" the reliability of a defensive system on which the future security of the United States may rest. There is a clear and present danger that scientists on both the inside and outside may become more interested in advocacy than in proof. Those based in Washington would do well to visit the Albert Einstein monument on the grounds of the National Academy of Science. Inscribed there is the standard they should all strive to reach: "The right to search for truth implies also a duty; one must not conceal any part of what one has recognized to be true."

Notes

1. *Washington Post,* January 26, 1985, p. A1; Kenneth Dam, *'Geneva and Beyond: New Arms Control Negotiations,'* Current Policy, No. 647 (Washington, D.C.: U.S. Department of State, Bureau of Public Affairs, January 14, 1985).

2. Defensive systems could be cost-effective at the margin in relation to offensive countermeasures, but still judged "unaffordable" in an unconstrained competition.

3. These criteria have been developed by a number of administration spokespeople. See, for example, *The President's Strategic Defense Initiative,* White House booklet, January 1985, p. 5; Lt. General James A. Abrahamson, *Statement on the SDI,* Committee on Armed Services, U.S. Senate, mimeo, February 21, 1985, p. 1; Ambassador Paul H. Nitze, *Statement before the Senate Foreign Relations Committee,* mimeo, February 26, 1985, p. 3; and U.S. Department of Defense, *Report to the Congress on the Strategic Defense Initiative,* 1985, p. 9.

4. Address before the American Astronautical Society, February 8, 1985.

5. This is not meant to minimize the operational uncertainties of launching large numbers of offensive weapons over distant and previously untested trajectories to their targets.

6. Senate Armed Services Committee, *Hearings on the Military Implications of the Treaty on the Limitations of Anti-Ballistic Missile Systems and the Interim Agreement on Limitation of Strategic Offensive Arms* (Washington, D.C.: U.S Government Printing Office, 1972), p. 377.

7. Quoted in *Pravda,* September 30,1972, pp. 1–2.

8. Quoted in *Aerospace Daily,* August 14, 1984, p. 242.

9. Representatives Norman Dicks and Albert Gore, Jr. threatened to prevent spending of any SDI funds that would erode the ABM Treaty. Their remarks followed a statement by National Security Advisor Robert McFarlane on "Meet the Press" (October 6, 1985) which indicated that the administration might feel legally free to test SDI technologies. Secretary of State George Shultz temporarily quieted the controversy in a speech before NATO Parliament members where he claimed that the president planned to observe the "traditional" interpretation of the treaty. The controversy is still very much alive, however, as evidenced by Assistant Secretary of Defense Richard Perle's telling reporters that any new work on strategic defense would be "weighed with the knowledge that we have the full legal right to act."

10. Peter Wyden, *Day One: Before Hiroshima and After* (New York: Simon and Schuster, 1984), pp. 38, 56.

4
Offensive Nuclear Forces, Strategic Defense, and Arms Control

O ffensive and defensive weapons with their supporting command and control networks form an integrated system for the conduct of nuclear war. Each part depends to some degree on the functioning of the other parts, and these interactions influence both the choice of weapons to deploy and the strategies for their employment. In the past, reducing the number of nuclear weapons and maintaining strategic stability required coordinated and parallel offensive–defensive constraints to minimize unilateral advantages and prevent unrestrained competition.[1]

The Reagan Strategic Defense Initiative has fundamentally altered previous efforts to engage in both offensive and defensive arms control negotiations, and instead views expanded strategic defenses and offensive-arms reductions as twin goals. Shifting from a strategic posture of offense-domination to defense-domination is filled with the uncertainties described in the preceding chapter. This chapter examines the strategic offensive–defensive relationship, current treaty commitments, and future negotiating strategies.

Offensive–Defensive Relationships

Arms control strategies aimed at achieving equal ceilings, attaining equal sublimits, or offsetting advantages in offensive weapons (for example, U.S. bomber or submarine-launched ballistic missile

(SLBM) advantages for Soviet ICBM advantages) may satisfy domestic political requirements and public perceptions of the strategic balance, but they do not necessarily support the operational effectiveness of nuclear forces if deterrence fails. This is not to suggest that war-fighting plans and strategies should drive arms control policy or vice versa. Nevertheless, strategic force levels codified by treaty will shape war-fighting options for the future, and the two must be related. Their credibility to deter war will depend to a large degree on the relationship between offensive trade-offs and defensive systems that may or may not be constrained by arms control agreements.

Table 4–1 illustrates possible relationships of offensive systems to defensive and offensive threats, defensive systems to offensive systems, and in the case of SDI technologies, potential offensive threats from "defensive" systems.

Examples from table 4–1 include:

1. Strategies designed to negotiate higher U.S. bomber limits to trade against Soviet ICBMs must take into account offensive threats to bomber bases and defensive (air defense) threats to bomber penetration.
2. Submarines must be able to survive offensive threats to their home ports and antisubmarine warfare (ASW) at sea, while their missiles must be able to penetrate Soviet missile defenses.
3. Space-based ballistic missile defenses can be attacked by antisatellite weapons and possibly ABMs. Space-based BMD systems must be able to defend themselves and therefore must have the ability to destroy ASATs. Limitations on ASATs may enhance the survivability of space-based defenses, but either side could circumvent treaty limitations by labelling an ASAT weapon as a BMD system or component. Conversely, BMD constraints could be circumvented by labelling a BMD weapon as an ASAT system or component. Because of their dual capabilities, both or neither should be constrained by treaty, but not one and not the other.
4. Similarly, space-based defenses could attack other space-based defenses. War in space could, therefore, begin with

Table 4–1
Strategic Nuclear Offensive–Defensive Linkages for U.S. Systems

Offensive System	Defensive Threat	Offensive Threat	Arms Control Remedies	Unilateral Remedies
1. Bombers	• Air Defense	• SLBMs and SLCMs • ICBMs	• SLCM Ban/Limitation • SSBN Patrol Area limits • Ban SLBM Depressed Trajectories • Air Defense Constraints	• ALCMs • Penetration Aids/Stealth Technology • Tactics • Higher Alert Rates • Basing Changes
2. ICBMs	• ABM Ground • BMD-Space	• ICBMs • SLBMs (Future)	• Launcher Limits • Missile Limits • Warhead Limits • Throw-weight Limits • ABM/BMD Constraints	• High Alert Rates • Hardening • C^3 Improvements • Launch Under Attack • Mobile ICBMs • Penetration Aids/MARVs
3. SSBNs/SLBMs (Submarines/Sub-launched ballistic missiles)	• ASW (Anti-Sub warfare) • ABM/BMD	• SLCMs • ICBMs (Threatens non-alert SSBNs) • SLBMs	• ABM/BMD Constraints • ASW Constraints • SSBN Sanctuaries • ICBM, SLCM, SLBM Constraints	• High Alert Rates • Technology/Stealth (Silence) • Penetration Aids/MARVs • Tactics • C^3
Defensive System				
4. ABM-Ground	• BMD-Space (Potential)	• MARV • Penetration Aids • Stealth Tech. • Cruise Missiles • EMP-Electro Magnetic pulse • Tactics/Mass	• BMD Constraints • MARV Constraints • Offensive Force Reductions	• Increase Assets • Harden System
5. BMD-Space	• ABM-Ground • BMD-Space • DSATs (Defensive Satellites)	• ASAT • Tactics/Mass • EMP, Blackout • ALCMs • GLCMs • SLCMs	• Ban BMD • Ban ASAT • Constrain: SLCM, GLCM, ALCM • Reduce Ballistic Missile Forces	• Increase Assets • Harden System • Tactics/Maneuver

preemptive attacks by "defensive" systems against defensive systems. Under such circumstances, battle stations would require escort vehicles or defensive satellites (DSATs) that could proliferate like components of a naval battle group around an aircraft carrier.

New technologies that may emerge from an unconstrained SDI could further obscure the offensive–defensive relationships depicted in table 4–1. If, for example, space-based "defenses" acquired a dual capability to destroy offensive weapons in flight and surface-based targets (such as ICBMs, ABMs, and ships), then "defensive" systems could not only support the offense indirectly by limiting a retaliatory attack, but could also support it directly through preemptive attacks against all targets. Explorations of new strategic frontiers promise a shield, but could deliver a sword as well.

These examples illustrate why nuclear arms control negotiations require a comprehensive, long-term approach to Soviet–American strategic capabilities. Treaties cannot embrace every possible threat or contingency, but neither should they result in vulnerable force structures because negotiatiors failed to comprehend the offensive–defensive relationships among strategic forces. It may also be worth noting potential unilateral remedies (table 4–1, column 5) or countermeasures that can be taken outside the context of an arms control treaty to shore-up U.S. defenses against evolving vulnerabilities or to strengthen our deterrent capabilities independent of treaty constraints. No treaty can lock all the doors to potential countermeasures.

Threats to strategic stability further complicate the distinction between offensive and defensive forces. If a large percentage of silo-based ICBMs, for example, could confidently ride out an attack, their offensive second-strike missions would be credible. But as fixed-based ICBMs become increasingly threatened, a use-them-or-lose-them or "defensive" preemption option becomes more attractive to a side with a countermilitary strategy.[2] When preemptive, damage-limiting attacks seem rational, strategic stability and deterrence considerations as conventionally defined vanish and distinctions between offensive and defensive roles and missions become blurred. Ideally, arms control agreements can promote strategic stability by reducing offensive forces to levels sufficiently low that deterrence can be achieved and maintained through unilateral programs such as mobile ICBMs, increased numbers of bombers on alert, and more submarines.

The maintenance of strategic stability is a major objective for arms control. The American approach to the problem has correctly been concentrated on reducing Soviet ICBMs. The insistence on distinguishing between fast-flying strategic forces (ballistic missiles) and slow-flying forces (bombers and cruise missiles) was initially a good strategy at Strategic Arms Reduction Talks (START). The United States attempted to negotiate major reductions in ballistic missiles, arguing that they were the most destabilizing systems given their short flight time, accuracy, high yields, and constant state of readiness. The Soviets (not unexpectedly since approximately 75 percent of their strategic warheads are deployed on land-based missiles) argued that all nuclear weapons were equally dangerous. Ballistic missiles rely on speed, while bombers and cruise missiles rely on stealth. Given Soviet force structure and predispositions for ICBMs, only treaty limits that can be aggregated in such a way that each party retains the freedom to mix strategic forces in its own way have any real chance of success.[3] For the Soviets this means protecting their considerable investment in land-based missiles.

The United States should continue to seek the reduction of Soviet ICBMs to their lowest possible levels, but without clinging to a nonnegotiable position that overdraws the saliency of the fast-flying–slow-flying distinction. Stability is largely a function of the ratio of hard-target–capable warheads to vulnerable counterforce targets in a preemptive attack. The more the ratio favors retaliatory forces, the greater the stability. Targeting ICBMs with ICBMs is not a solution to the problem of strategic stability. Bombers and cruise missiles can perform second-strike, counterforce missions if it is agreed that the only rationale (compatible with strategic stability) for strategic counterforce targeting is to preclude reloading of silos and retention of reserves. If the Soviets strike first, there is no reason why they could not be as prepared to launch any withheld missiles on short warning of retaliatory ICBMs as they would be on longer warning of approaching bombers armed with cruise missiles. Moreover, if the United States reduces its own ICBMs (and/or deploys mobile ICBMs) to expand bomber and cruise missile forces, it would reduce Soviet counterforce capability by trimming the target base against which ICBMs are useful.[4]

Employment policies that are compatible with strategic stability could be achieved if American negotiators can exact favorable bomber-for-ICBM trade-offs. This could be done either through unequal, but offsetting limitations on bombers, bomber weapons, missiles, and warheads or through aggregating total counterforce capability with less emphasis on fast versus slow-flying delivery vehicles. The Soviets may find such trade-offs to be an acceptable way of protecting their investment in heavy ICBMs from sudden, arms-control–dictated changes. "Sudden" is the key word in this context, since over time, the vulnerability of fixed, land-based missiles may drive the Soviets to more survivable mobile ICBMs. The technological requirements of mobile ICBMs could indirectly move Soviet forces toward the U.S. objective of reducing the number of heavy missiles and the number of warheads each is capable of carrying.[5]

Formal Treaty Linkages between Offensive and Defensive Systems

SALT I formally linked offensive and defensive forces in the arms control process. The ABM Treaty and the *Interim* Agreement or SALT I (emphasis added on "Interim") rest on the assumption that limiting strategic defense would reduce first-strike incentives and contributed to a more stable deterrence. The United States expected that limitations on defensive forces would reduce the requirements for Soviet offensive forces. The inability to limit multiple independently targeted reentry vehicles (MIRVs) in SALT I, however, guaranteed that attempts to drive down Soviet offensive forces through defensive limits would fail. Whether through strategic design or imitation, it was certain that in the absence of treaty constraints on U.S. systems, the Soviets would follow the American lead with MIRV deployments of their own. The results created, for the first time, a convergence of Soviet strategic doctrine with a theoretical capability to execute it. (See figure 4–1.)

The permissive nature of SALT I and the slow pace of follow-

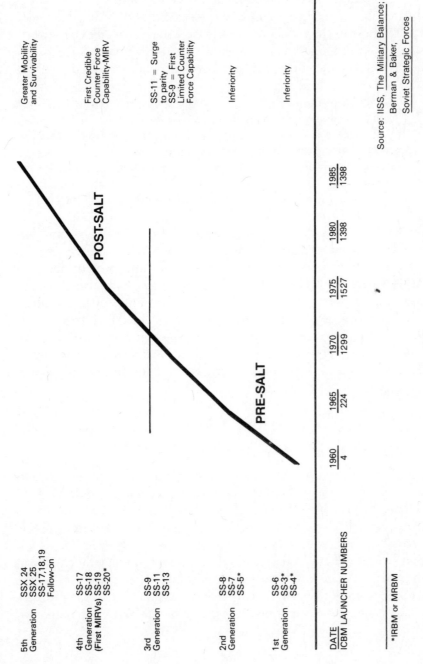

Figure 4–1. *Soviet Strategic Evolution—ICBMs*

on negotiations leave reductions in offensive forces as the most enduring objective of arms control. The ABM Treaty codified the need for progress in the reduction of offensive nuclear weapons. Ambassador Smith's unilateral statement of understanding of this requirement added a specific time frame (five years) and stressed:

> The US Delegation believes that an objective of the follow-on negotiations should be to constrain and reduce on a long-term basis threats to the survivability of our respective strategic retaliatory forces. If an agreement providing for more complete strategic offensive arms limitations were not achieved within five years, US supreme interests could be jeopardized. Should that occur, it would constitute a basis for withdrawal from the ABM Treaty.[6]

SALT II placed a ceiling on the growth of offensive systems, but at levels higher than those anticipated by SALT I strategists who attempted to gain Soviet offensive constraints indirectly through the ABM Treaty. As Ambassador Smith's statement makes clear, the Soviets were put on notice at SALT I that the failure of this strategy would constitute grounds for abrogation of the ABM Treaty. This long-standing position of linking defensive constraints to offensive reductions, combined with the president's Strategic Defense Initiative, will continue to play a crucial role in future bargaining strategy.

Negotiating Strategy and SDI

The Soviets are obviously concerned about future programs that may emerge under the rubric of SDI. This concern could provide leverage for the United States if we are willing to accept constraints at reasonably early stages in the development of ballistic missile defenses. The Soviets have made it clear in every negotiating forum that the president's initiative would create a fundamental change in the Soviet–American strategic relationship. A succession of Soviet leaders from Andropov to Gorbachev have charged that the purpose of the new conception represented by the SDI in combination with strategic modernization programs, is to give the United States strategic superiority. In the first official Soviet response, Yuri Andropov argued that the ABM Treaty had established:

> an inseverable interconnection between strategic offensive and defense weapons. Only mutual restraint in the field of ABM defense will allow progress in limiting and reducing offensive weapons. Today, however, the United States intends to sever this interconnection and open the floodgates of a runaway race of all types of strategic arms.[7]

Konstantin Chernenko publicly announced that future arms control talks would cover "the entire complex of interconnected questions of the nonmilitarization of outer space, reductions of strategic nuclear arms, and medium range nuclear weapons."[8] Chernenko's call for talks on the "entire complex of interconnected questions" paralleled Reagan's earlier U.N. speech that called for "umbrella talks" on wide-ranging arms issues.[9] That trial balloon was viewed inside the government as a general appeal that would avoid a showdown between conflicting agencies and bureaus over the substance of U.S. arms control policies. According to the director of the Arms Control and Disarmament Agency, these umbrella talks would be high-level discussions that would sort out the agenda for future Soviet–American arms control negotiations.[10]

The negotiating agenda and a new long-range strategic concept were partially defined during the January 1985 meetings in Geneva between Secretary of State Shultz and former foreign minister Gromyko. Both parties agreed to three sets of negotiations—strategic nuclear weapons, theater nuclear forces, and space/defense. There was also agreement that the three negotiating forums were interrelated, but the precise nature of their linkage set off a controversy that has persisted throughout the negotiations themselves. The United States expressed the hope that progress in one set of negotiations could be implemented if it were in the interests of both sides. Soviet leaders, by contrast, saw progress in talks to ban space weapons as "inseparable" from the question of dealing with strategic and medium-range nuclear arms.

The disagreement over sequential or simultaneous progress is rooted in Soviet apprehension about SDI. The Soviet preference for simultaneous progress in all negotiating forums was made explicit by Gromyko, who informed his Soviet audience during a televised Moscow news conference that "the three directions during the conduct of the negotiations naturally increase the number of different components, and possibilities for their exchange and different adjustments are growing."[11] Gromyko's apparent invitation to bargain and the manner in which the United States has structured its negotiating team (Ambassador Kampelman leads the space negotiations and is titular head of all the negotiations) will facilitate future trade-offs and linkages among the three sets of negotiations.

If operational linkages exist between offense and defense, then offensive and defensive weapons should not be uncoupled for purposes of arms control. For the United States in the near term, the broader the agenda and the greater the linkage between offensive-defensive forces, the greater the negotiating leverage. Our negotiators may be in a position to trade SDI constraints for both Soviet offensive-force reductions and matching Soviet ABM constraints. Arms control leverage and bargaining strength, however, are time-sensitive commodities with a short shelf-life. If the Soviets match our SDI initiatives or break out of the ABM Treaty, we will find our bargaining parameters narrowed to trading defensive constraints for defensive constraints. The opportunity for rolling offensive missile reductions into the bargain will have been substantially reduced, if not lost.

The issue of offensive–defensive trade-offs in the negotiations has been made more complex by the larger issue introduced by the United States in the form of a "new strategic concept." (See chapter 6 for a more detailed account.) Reportedly drafted by Paul Nitze, the new U.S. concept links the goal of deep cuts in offensive weapons with the development of strategic defenses over a long, carefully phased transition period. During the next ten years the United States will seek a radical reduction (build-down) in offensive nuclear arms, followed by a period of mutual transition to effective nonnuclear defense forces as technology makes such options available. In a final "ultimate period" (defined as deterrence based on the ability to deny success to an attacker) strategic defenses could make it possible to eliminate all nuclear weapons.[12]

The Soviets made it clear during the Gromyko–Shultz meeting that they reject the new strategic concept, and are not interested in turning the negotiations into a protracted seminar or tutorial on the virtues of strategic defense. The real issue behind the debate over sequential or simultaneous progress in the three negotiating forums is whether the United States is willing to bargain future SDI constraints on testing and development in exchange for deep reductions in offensive forces.

The START–SDI relationship may be the most difficult to reconcile, because of the efforts required to explore new technological frontiers in the offensive–defensive relationship and the impact of those explorations on existing arms control treaties. In the near term, extensive research may increase Soviet incentives to negotiate new agreements and comply with existing ones. More certainly, R&D could eventually provide insurance against a sudden Soviet strategic breakthrough or long-term unilateral advantages gained through noncompliance or treaty abrogation. These issues are complicated by divisions within the Reagan administration. Some officials want to use SDI as negotiating leverage; others seek to protect it from all forms of arms-control-dictated constraints.[13] The debate is complicated even among the pro-arms control faction by questions of how far you can go in "demonstrating" a new technology before violating existing agreements, and how one gets newly demonstrated technologies to the bargaining table without precipitating Soviet countermeasures.

By the late 1980s, pressure will almost certainly mount (in proportion to funds expended) to test or demonstrate the new technologies that are expected to provide defense against ballistic missiles. At that point, decisions will have to be made about future ABM Treaty compliance.

Three major options seem the most likely:

1. Hold off testing ballistic missile defense technologies until all efforts to negotiate reductions in Soviet offensive forces have been exhausted.

2. Negotiate ABM Treaty modifications with the Soviets that would allow testing of BMD components and new technologies.
3. Exercise the right to abrogate the ABM Treaty and move ahead with full-scale testing and deployment of BMD.

The first option is the most desirable for the future of a stable arms control regime. However, uncertain progress in both our own and Soviet development of ballistic missile defense makes it difficult to assess our leverage for SDI–START trade-offs. For a virtual catch-22, the amount of leverage is tied to demonstrated capability being negotiated away, but those demonstrations can only be made outside treaty restrictions.

The Soviets are not likely to agree on ABM Treaty amendments (option 2) if they think our research programs are further advanced than their own or if they believe that those programs can be constrained by United States domestic politics. The Soviets could drag out the negotiations for such amendments in the attempt to delay and kill United States programs. They could (instead of or in addition to such delays) refuse to agree to such amendments, giving Washington the unhappy choice of either halting its programs under Soviet pressure or withdrawing from the ABM Treaty (and thus being subject to criticism that the United States had torpedoed the treaty). The latter could fit Soviet interests if they were ready to begin deployment of a large-scale traditional ABM system, while the United States was still some years away from an advanced BMD, or even state-of-the-art deployment, or possibly even a decision to deploy.

Abrogation of the ABM Treaty (option 3) has the same serious political consequence, and would make it difficult for the president to achieve the major goal of his SDI—to decrease reliance on offensive nuclear forces.

In the long term, if ballistic missile defense becomes technically feasible and cost-effective, the Soviets may find that the value of ballistic missiles is reduced, which may increase the chances of negotiated reductions. Alternatively, and more likely in the short term, they may develop active (offensive) and passive (defensive) countermeasures to future defensive systems.

SDI and Soviet Countermeasures

SDI and its related research and development programs are aimed at producing a multilayered, multitechnological approach to ballistic missile defenses. Attacking ballistic missiles in each phase of their flight with weapons that destroy them in different ways forces the offense to attempt the difficult task of overcoming various threats.[14] (See figure 4–2.)

The earliest or boost phase of a missile's flight segment starts from launch and extends only from two to five minutes into flight. During this time a missile produces an extremely intense heat or infrared signal that can be picked up by space-based detection and warning systems. Because the missile is carrying all its nuclear warheads, decoys, and penetration aids, it is a very high value target for the defense. The capability of interception is critical for a credible layered defense system.[15] Unfortunately, during the first 200,000 feet of a missile's ascent it is relatively immune from attack either because United States defenses may not be able to react quickly enough to attack the missile earlier or because many defensive technologies cannot penetrate deeply into the Earth's atmosphere from their space-based orbits. For these reasons many scientists are not optimistic that reliable boost-phrase intercepts are possible with any technology visible on the horizon.

The second or postboost phase occurs after the missile's first stages have burned out and fallen away from the postboost vehicle (PBV) or "bus" which carries the warheads and decoys. The warheads and decoys are released during a sequence of small, controlled maneuvers. The bus generates small infrared bursts of energy as it maneuvers, and it is, therefore, still detectable from space-based sensors. However, once warheads, chaff, decoys, and other objects are released, detection becomes far more difficult. The postboost vehicle, therefore, is a high-value target that quickly declines in value as it launches each of its warheads on separate trajectories to their targets.

During the third or midcourse phase, lasting fifteen to twenty minutes, the released warheads and decoys follow their predetermined trajectories. Discrimination between threatening and non-threatening objects by defensive sensors is made difficult by the po-

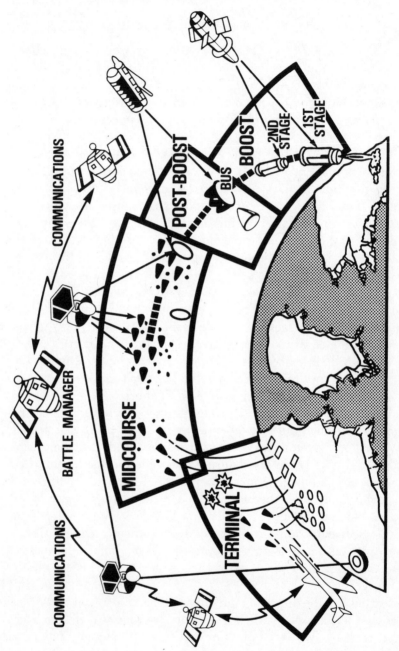

COMMUNICATIONS

POST-BOOST

BOOST

2ND STAGE

1ST STAGE

BUS

COMMUNICATIONS

BATTLE MANAGER

MIDCOURSE

TERMINAL

COMMUNICATIONS

Figure 4–2. *Layered Defense Concept*

tentially large number of decoys that could be deployed. Detection is further complicated by the fact that warheads and decoys cool rapidly to a temperature very close to that of the surrounding space, making it difficult for infrared sensors to acquire and hold any target, much less distinguish nuclear warheads from thousands of other objects, and fire on them in the relatively short period of time involved.

During the final reentry phase, the warheads reenter the atmosphere. Detection again becomes comparatively easy because of the heat generated during reentry and because lightweight decoys and chaff burn up. Unfortunately, reentry lasts only thirty to one hundred seconds. Detection and interception must take place almost instantly to avoid offensive–defensive dueling literally overhead.

These technical challenges will face defense advocates even if the Soviets play the role of cooperative adversary. The latter is not likely, and prudent planners will have to anticipate a variety of Soviet countermeasures. Several of these have already been identified in United States studies and by the Soviets themselves.[16] Table 4–2 summarizes many that strategic defenses will be required to overcome, including:

Proliferation of missiles and warheads to exhaust defenses in each phase or layer.

Reflective coatings and spin boosters to serve as protection from lasers.

Increased thrust and/or reduced payload to reduce boost phase to less than one minute.

Deployment of ASATs, including space mines, to degrade space-based defenses. (As Robert DeGrasse and Stephen Daggett have pointed out, the ultimate cost and complexity of a space-based system may be affected by the need to defend itself from preemptive attack. Like aircraft carriers, the cost of protecting the primary assets may exceed the price of the firepower the system delivers.)[17]

Table 4–2
Countermeasures to Advanced Ballistic Missile Defenses

TRAJECTORY PHASE	HARDENING	DECOY	DATA DENIAL	EXHAUST	EVADE	ATTACK DEFENSE
Boost	• Coatings: Ablative Reflective • Spin Booster	• Dummy Boosters • Smoke/Flare Generators	• Jam with ground-based systems • Camouflage • Smoke	• Mass Attacks • Increase Payload • Mobile Basing	• Fast Burn Boosters • Depressed trajectories	• ASAT • Space mine
Post Boost	• Harden bus, • Single RV missiles		• Mask with Aerosols	• Multiple buses	• Fast burn buses	• ASAT • Space mine
Midcourse	• Harden RVs against X-rays	• Chaff • Baloons • Optical & LWIR Decoys (Long Wave Infrared)	• Aerosols • Radar & optical jamming	• MiRVs		• ASAT • Space Mine
Terminal		• Optical, radar & LWIR decoys	• Optical & radar jamming	• MiRVs	• MaRV • Salvage Fusing • Cruise Missiles • Stealth Technology	• Precursor Attacks

Deployment of thousands of decoys or chaff to avoid midcourse detection. (This includes the use of masking aerosols and hiding warheads inside specially constructed balloons to make them indistinguishable from decoys.)

Maneuverable warheads (MaRV) to evade terminal defenses.

The viability of each Soviet countermeasure is, like SDI technologies, subject to debate and the assumptions of various studies and advocates. Nevertheless, if only a few of the many responses available to the offense are feasible, deployment of defensive systems will have to be very cost effective at the start to overcome domestic opposition.

A vigorous SDI program is not only likely to be expensive, but it could undercut efforts to get reductions in ballistic missiles, and could also trigger new and unconstrained competition in both offensive and defensive systems. Certainly the United States could not risk neglecting its offensive forces in the face of massive Soviet offensive countermeasures to BMD programs. The evolution of American technologies to counter those countermeasures may be possible, but only at correspondingly increased system complexity and cost. And even these defensive counters will be just one more step in the never ending contest between offense and defense.

Attempts to constrain the offensive–defensive competition forecast by critics will be complicated by many uncertainties. Efforts to limit defensive weapons and related counting rules required by both present and future arms control regimes will be obscured by as yet unanswered and undefined technical questions. For example, how many satellites will be required to defend against a growing Soviet offense. (See chapter 3.) What are their rates or volume of fire, their sustainability, their forms of energy regeneration, and/or the reload/reconstitution capabilities of the various space and ground-based systems under R&D? Answers to these basic questions are critical to any assessment of the system's cost-effectiveness or its capability of staying ahead of offensive countermeasures.[18] The technical and economic feasibility of the transition to a defense-dominant world cannot be known until technical developments make clear choices of systems possible. The ABM–START–SDI dilemma is that answers to the questions of systems, force levels, and capabilities probably cannot be learned in an environment where previous arms control agreements have survived or where new agreements are being negotiated.

As these and other SDI issues spill into public debate, offensive–defensive interactions will become increasingly visible and divisive. As they do, they are likely to undermine the president's major selling point—that defensive systems can decrease reliance on offensive nuclear weapons. This is especially true in the face of conflicting statements on SDI's mission in strategic policy. The president has repeatedly described SDI as a step leading to the total defense of the American people. Secretary of Defense Weinberger went further in describing SDI as "morally right" since "it is an attempt to devise a system that protects our people instead of avenging them."[19]

Virtually no one closely associated with defensive technologies, however, believes that a leakproof system required for defending the American urban population is likely. Strategic defense can protect the deterrent force and decrease incentives for an attack on the United States. This is the most desirable and credible mission for SDI, and it should be clearly stated as part of the debate. Fred Ikle, undersecretary of defense, defined the mission of a defensive system in precisely these terms when he revealed that the administration might build an interim system that would protect nuclear missiles, but not cities.[20] When so stated, defensive technologies can be more readily contrasted with arms control as an alternative to reducing the Soviet offensive threat.

Finally, it becomes essential to view United States SDI and strategic modernization programs as part of a single strategy that feeds Soviet strategic planning. As long as our strategic modernization program includes unconstrained hard target systems—MX, D-5, and possibly cruise missiles—the Soviets will have few incentives to reduce their offensive weapons. The ultimate "layered" defense may include the capability to destroy a high percentage of Soviet ICBMs in their silos or support bases (in the case of mobile ICBMs). The deployment of interim defenses makes the threat from modernized offensive systems all the more credible. As long as the Soviets confront the dual threats of strategic modernization programs and SDI with interim stages, there will be little chance of achieving the pres-

ident's goal of moving toward a defense-dominant world while negotiating offensive-arms reductions. These twin goals are hopelessly
in conflict.

SDI as an Arms Control Dilemma

SDI also faces considerable domestic and international political difficulty. Domestically, timely and adequate funding from Congress
will confront a maze of contentious economic, technical, strategic,
and arms control debates during which SDI must enjoy technological successes and a sustained political consensus to maintain costly,
multiyear programs. Internationally, the viability of SDI will depend
on United States ability to limit offensive weapons. SDI and arms
control must, therefore, be carefully coordinated rather than made
to appear antithetical. An arms control strategy that coordinates
offensive and defensive systems requires the preservation of the ne-
gotiation process to provide a forum for reducing the level of offensive nuclear weapons. This will almost certainly require the continuation of interim restraint (abiding by SALT I and II ceilings) on
offensive arms and nonabrogation of the ABM Treaty. This, in turn,
will require a clear commitment to accept future constraints on SDI
testing and deployments.

Offensive–defensive coordination would also require major re-
visions in previous START proposals. Despite considerable rhetoric
about deep cuts (50 percent reductions), both sides have attempted
to protect very large numbers of offensive weapons. The initial ceilings proposed at START in 1983 were so high and the prohibitions
on specific weapons so few that both sides' positions were designed
to support an offensive-dominant world, and thus were inconsistent
with more recent movement in Washington toward strategic defense. If the United States wishes to encourage effective defenses,
for instance, it must discourage such things as:

1. MaRVs as a principal means of penetrating terminal ABMs;
2. Air- and sea-launched cruise missiles requiring large and
   costly air defense systems;
3. The proliferation of new types of ballistic missiles that would

facilitate the development of countermeasures to SDI (fast-burn boosters, reflective coatings, spin boosters);

4. High ceilings for sea-launched ballistic missiles, since the position uncertainty and short flight times make defense against them difficult;

5. ASAT testing and deployments, since they are major threats to command control, communication, and intelligence (C^3I), battle management, and satellite battle stations.

Limiting offensive–defensive competition requires mutually balanced constraints. Ascendancy on one side of the equation by either party is certain to provoke short-term countermeasures on the other side and long-term competition in both offensive and defensive technologies. Negotiating leverage and willingness to accept constraints in both offense and defense are two sides of the same coin. Failure to compromise will surely result in a Soviet effort to match United States defenses. Mutual fear that the other side may develop offensive means to penetrate defenses will fuel competition in both. These are the strategic hurdles to reaching the president's goal of offensive reductions in a defense-dominant world. Arms control that includes both defensive and offensive constraints—as well as including unilateral basing and deployment solutions to the problems of weapons vulnerability—offers the most cost-effective and stable answers to the twin problems facing strategic forces—survivability and penetrability.

This, in essence, was the conclusion of the Scowcroft Commission Report endorsed by the president on April 29, 1983.[21] The bipartisan report recommended the deployment of a small, mobile ICBM, smaller and more numerous submarines, improved communications, and increased penetration effectiveness of retaliatory forces. These steps are more likely to lead to successful arms control negotiations and strategic stability than the offensive–defensive arms competition that is likely to grow out of the president's Strategic Defensive Initiative.

Long-term strategic stability as defined here requires arms control stability. Arms control stability grows out of an environment of formal constraints and well-defined force structures in both offensive and defensive systems that are sufficiently secure that neither side feels compelled to deploy new systems to match or offset the deployments of the other. Strategic stability and arms control stability are indivisible. Strategic stability without arms control is a temporary and fragile posture threatened by a constantly changing strategic landscape.

Notes

1. Strategic stability is defined here as a condition of the military balance that, in a crisis, offers the Soviet Union no incentive to initiate a nuclear attack. Neither is the United States under pressure to do so. By contrast, strategic instability would be a condition in which either the United States or the Soviet Union (or both) believed that victory could be achieved and defeat averted only by striking the other side preemptively.

2. The Department of Defense specifically rejects such a strategy for the United States. The Soviets through former minister of defense Dimitri Ustinov and Griorgi Arbotov, head of the Institute for the Study of the United States and Canada, have stated they might move toward a strategy of launch-on-warning if their land-based missiles became vulnerable to a preemptive strike. See *Washington Post*, April 11, 1982, p. 5, and *Los Angeles Times*, July 18, 1982, p. 3E.

3. Discussed in Strobe Talbot, *Deadly Gambits* (New York: Alfred A. Knoff, 1984), p. 282.

4. This point is made by Richard K. Betts in "Elusive Equivalence: The Political and Military Meaning of the Military Balance" in *The Strategic Imperative,* ed. Samuel Huntington (Cambridge, Mass.: Ballinger, 1982), p. 126. The concept also assumes that in a protracted nuclear war, the United States could maintain an intelligence capability to "see" Soviet targets and distinguish empty from unfired silos.

5. United States bomber and cruise missile advantages that offset Soviet ICBM advantages will, as table 4–1 indicates, depend on the continued penetrability of U.S. Forces. Unconstrained Soviet modernization of air defenses will, at some point, make this trade-off unattractive. The reverse could also be true with unconstrained United States ballistic missile defenses.

6. *Arms Control and Disarmament Agreements* (Washington, D.C.: U.S. Arms Control and Disarmament Agency, 1982), p. 146.

7. *Pravda*, March 27, 1983, p. 1.

8. *Washington Post*, November 27, 1984, p. A15.

9. Text quoted in *New York Times*, September 25, 1984, p. A10.

10. Kenneth Adelman, quoted in *Washington Post*, November 8, 1984, p. A40.

11. For the text of Gromyko's news conference, see Foreign Broadcast Information Service, *USSR International Affairs*, United States Information Agency, Janu-

ary 14, 1985, pp. 1–16. Gromyko's remarks quoted here were also carried in a commentary by Vladimir Bogachev in *Tass,* January 14, 1985.

12. The "new strategic concept" was first made public in a little noticed speech to the Foreign Policy Association by Deputy Secretary of State Kenneth W. Dam, *Geneva and Beyond: New Arms Control Negotiations, Current Policy,* No. 647 (United States Department of State, Bureau of Public Affairs, January 14, 1985). Ambasador Nitze further developed the concept in a speech before the Philadelphia World Affairs Council on February 20, 1985, and in his testimony before the Senate Foreign Relations Committee on February 26, 1985. Cynics have already noted that Nitze's "ultimate period" in which nuclear weapons wither away is matched in its idealism only by the Marxist–Leninist theory of the "withering away" of the state.

13. The president's science advisor, George Keyworth, called space-based defenses "inevitable" (*Baltimore Sun,* September 18, 1984, p. 1). Undersecretary of Defense Fred Ikle has stated, "the US should not trade its "star wars" research program for reductions in Soviet nuclear missiles" (Quoted in *Washington Post,* October 27, 1984, A16). Ambassador Rowny has favored demonstrating the technical feasibility of Star Wars before attempting to trade it against Soviet offensive reductions. Lt. General James Abrahamson, head of the strategic defense organization at the Department of Defense, has suggested a three-year deployment delay in exchange for a reduction of five hundred Soviet warheads (*Christian Science Monitor,* October 29, 1984, p. 3). In a *New York Times* interview on February 12, 1985, and during his send-off speech to the United States delegation on March 8, 1985, the president stressed that the United States would not negotiate limits on SDI research, a position by which he stands. Deployment of strategic defenses however, has never been specifically ruled out of current or future negotiations.

14. The layered defense concept is described in *Directed Energy Missile Defense In Space—A Background Paper* (Washington, D.C.: United States Congress, Office of Technology Assessment, 1984); *The Fallacy of Star Wars* ed. John Tirman (New York: Vintage, 1984), chaps. 5–6; Sidney Drell, Philip J. Farley, and David Holloway, "Preserving the ABM Treaty: A Critique of the Reagan Strategic Defense Initiative," *International Security* 9, no. 2 (Fall1984):67–83; *Defense against Ballistic Missiles: An Assessment of Technologies and Policies Implications* (Washington, D.C.: United States Department of Defense, March 6, 1984); and Leon Sloss, "The Return of Strategic Defense," *Strategic Review,* 12 (Summer 1984):37–44.

15. George Keyworth told a group of aerospace executives that boost-phase intercept is the most important challenge in SDI, that it is the "hinge" of all other work. Quoted in *Aerospace Daily,* May 22, 1985, p. 123.

16. For example, from note 14, Office of Technology Assessment, 45–54, and Tirman, 21–26. The Soviets have also openly discussed countermeasures. See, for example, Committee of Soviet Scientists for Peace against Nuclear War, "Strategic and International Political Consequences of Creating a Space-Based

Anti-missile System Using Directed Energy Weapons" (paper presented at the Meeting of Delegates of the United States National Academy of Sciences and the Academy of Sciences of the USSR on Problems of International Security and Arms Control, Moscow, May 8–11, 1984), pp. 21–26. It should also be noted that Soviet sources which emphasize countermeasures against SDI have great propaganda value, and should not be taken as official Soviet views on the real technological potential of SDI research.

17. William D. Hartung, Robert W. DeGrasse Jr., Rosy Nimroody, Stephen Daggett, and Jeb Bragman, *The Strategic Defense Initiative: Costs, Contractors, and Consequences* (New York: The Council on Economic Priorities, 1985), p. 18.

18. According to testimony by James A. Thomason, director of the National Security Strategies Program at the RAND Corporation, the offense will have an advantage under all circumstances. A strategy for deterrence that relies solely on the defense's ability to deny damage to a determined Soviet attacker is beyond our reach. Testimony before the Defense Appropriations Subcommittee of the House Appropriations Committee, May 9,1984.

19. Speech before the Pittsburgh World Affairs Council, United States Department of Defense press release, October 20, 1984.

20. *Washington Post,* October 27, 1984, p. A16. "Interim" defense means defense of ICBM sites against the terminal phase of an ICBM attack. See *Defense against Ballistic Missiles: An Assessment of Technology and Policy Implications* (Washington D.C.: United States Department of Defense, 1984), p. 8.

21. *President's Commission on Strategic Forces,* report of March 21, 1984, mimeo, pp. 9, 11, 20, 21.

5
New Technologies versus Old Tactics

The History of Offensive–Defensive Relationships

Historically, the evolution from a period of offensive dominance to one of defensive dominance and back has occurred through technological innovation or tactical adaptation. There are no examples of negotiated transitions. Recognition of the historical shifts from offensive and defensive dominance may be instructive for the current SDI debate. The United States objective of freeing Soviet–American relations from the threat of nuclear war is not the first attempt to break out of an offense-dominated world.

The offensive–defensive cycles that have directed the course of warfare throughout history may serve to caution proponents of SDI against undue optimism about technology's potential to create a permanent revolution in strategic capabilities. (See table 5–1.) If history has lessons for us, surely one is that a transition to strategic defense will not only be a technical problem, but also a posture that will require maintenance and considerable resources over time.

SDI could do for the United States what conventional fortifications did for European cities—make a high-value target less attractive. But just as the most elaborate fortifications were eventually overcome by the application of greater firepower and assault capabilities, strategic defenses will be vulnerable if there are no limits on Soviet offensive forces.

Even before fortresses were penetrable, the strategic defense of European cities spawned marauding armies which roamed the field

Table 5–1
Historical Patterns of Offensive–Defensive Dominance

	Supporting Military Technology and Tactics
1200–1450	
Defensive superiority	Fortifications outpaced destructive power of weapons and siege tactics
	Plate armor reduced mobility
	English longbow improved tactical defense and made it difficult for offense to close
1450–1525	
Offensive superiority	Artillery made medieval fortifications obsolete
	New small firearms were more effective than pike and armor
	Mobility and lighter weapons stressed
1525–1650	
Experts divided	Some experts see resurgence of fortifications over offensive force
1650–1740	
Defensive superiority	New science of fortifications and military engineering made defense against artillery and frontal attack possible
1789–1815	
Offensive superiority	Napoleonic period emphasized mobility and offensive tactics
	Mass mobilization
	Efficient use of weapons and tactics were emphasized more than technological innovation
1815–1850	
Period of relative European peace	
1850–1925	
Defensive superiority	Use of entrenchments, barbed wire, machine gun, and breech loading rifle
	Tank used as protected fire support
1930s–1945	
Offensive superiority	Armored divisions
	Tanks in the offensive
	Close air support

Table 5–1
Continued

Supporting Military Technology and Tactics
Speed, deep penetration, and broad encirclement
Strategic bombing

1945–1980s	
Offensive superiority	Evolution of nuclear deterrence
	Strategic nuclear weapons
	Defense by threat of offensive retaliation
	Theater nuclear weapons[a]
	Tactical nuclear weapons[a]
	Wars of national liberation
	Terrorism
1990s–2000	
?	Policies determined by:
	Technology
	Resources
	Political will
	Tactics and strategy
	Arms control

Source: Compiled from: Bernard and Fawn Brodie, *From Crossbow to H-Bomb* (Bloomington, IN: Indiana University Press, 1973); Quincy Wright, *A Study of War* (Chicago: University of Chicago Press, 1965); J.F.C. Fuller, *Armament and History* (New York: Charles Scribner and Sons, 1945); Jack S. Levy, "The Offensive/Defensive Balance of Military Technology: A Theoretical and Historical Analysis," *International Studies Quarterly* 28, no. 2 (June 1984): 219–238.

[a]These weapons also have defensive missions against conventional formations massed for attack.

at will. Governments that invested their resources in fortresses could not sortie against those armies unless they could also afford to build and maintain an appropriate offensive force. Otherwise, those who lived in surrounding villages (in the case of SDI, Europeans) got little protection once deterrence failed.

Throughout history, military technology has been exploited to *penetrate* enemy defenses or to *blunt* enemy attacks. From medieval castles, armor-clad soldiers, and Maginot lines to mobile artillery, tank offensives, and strategic bombing, the pendulum has swung from offensive advantages to defensive advantages and back again.

Military technology has never succeeded in freezing this dynamic relationship. One reason for this should be easy to understand. Science is neutral. Technological innovation works with equal force on both sides of the offensive–defensive equation. This can be seen today if we contrast the technological research in the SDI program with our own offensive strategic modernization programs which include:

Maneuverable warheads for ICBMs

Stealth technology for bombers and cruise missiles

Large numbers of sea-launched cruise missiles on submarines and surface ships

Active and passive penetration aids for missiles and bombers

ASATs, which are offensive in their mission against space-based defense systems

Most of these same programs can be found in some stage of Soviet research and development. Together, they accelerate the evolution of countermeasures that may put our defensive goals out of reach. In a sense, this is what happened from the late 1960s to the present when Soviet state-of-the art ABM systems and air defenses contributed to the deployment of U.S. MIRVed missiles, air-launched cruise missiles, and stand-off bombers.

These examples of concurrent research and development in offensive and defensive systems illustrate how the accelerated pace of military technology in the nuclear era has made the lessons of previous periods—periods dominated by land warfare—less valid for strategic planners. Strategies for land warfare, for example, can still postulate the offensive requirements for defeating an adversary on a particular front (for example, a 3:1 force ratio for an offensive against NATO). No such guidelines have emerged for nuclear weapons. Problems of massive destruction, massive preemption versus limited attack options, and hard-target counterforce versus countervalue targeting obscure such facile offensive–defensive ratios. The "fog and friction" of war which Clausewitz described more than a century ago is still relevant to modern warfare. High technology and nuclear weapons open the parameters of uncertainty even wider than those faced by individual soldiers and military planners who struggled in the nineteenth century wars from which Clausewitz drew his analysis.

Through their public statements since the Star Wars speech, the Soviets have made it clear that they are unwilling participants in any future and historically unique diplomatic transition to a world dominated by strategic defense. Preventing deployment of weapons in space is clearly their current major objective, and they have linked progress in offensive arms negotiations to limits on strategic defense in space.

The Soviets are obviously concerned about future programs that may emerge from SDI. If arms control negotiations fail and the United States proceeds unilaterally with unconstrained development and deployment of strategic defenses, there are many potential offensive countermeasures available to Soviet planners. They are likely to develop the most cost-effective combination of technological innovations and tactical adaptations to the task of countering the political–military effects of U.S. strategic defenses. Technological countermeasures (such as fast-burn boosters, spin boosters, MaRVs, and ASATs) have been treated extensively elsewhere and summarized in the previous chapter.[1] Tactical adaptation, however, has received far less attention. This chapter focuses on three possible areas of tactical adaptation to strategic defense: massing of ballistic missile forces to penetrate space-based defenses, circumvention through bombers and cruise missiles, and conventional superiority in Europe.

Massing of Ballistic Missile Forces

The political viability of strategic defense in the United States will ultimately depend on costs and cost-exchange ratios between defensive and offensive countermeasures. The technological and strategic viability of SDI, as currently defined, depends on developing reliable boost-phase intercept capabilities. The dilemma faced by the scientific community is that costs cannot be determined or limited

through technology alone. In the absence of offensive limits or reductions, the Soviets will play a major role in determining the costs
of United States defenses through their countermeasures against
boost-phase defense.

Space-based defenses against ballistic missiles in their boost
phase must be dispersed to protect against Soviet deployments of
offensive missiles across the full breadth of the Soviet Union and at
sea. Estimates for the number of satellite battle stations required to
counter these threats have varied widely from several hundred to
less than one hundred depending on often unstated assumptions
about technical performance, Soviet countermeasures, and the type
of weapons being described. The one feature common to most estimates is that they are based on current Soviet ICBM deployments
(fourteen hundred) and ignore a dispersed submarine threat.

The methodological battle over the calculation of these numbers remains intense. Consensus on methodology, however, will not
close the debate. Satellite numbers must also be responsive to unknown Soviet countermeasures. Here, the offense has a tactical advantage, since it can disperse its forces at sea while massing them
on land through additional deployments of silo-based and mobile
ICBMs (both road and rail-mobile ICBMs are probable) to concentrate attacks in the traditional style of Soviet military doctrine. The
map in figure 5–1 shows the possible concentrations that could be
massed with existing Soviet forces.

Without offensive constraints, current ICBM concentrations
could grow and be further reinforced during a crisis by rail-mobile
ICBMs to confront defensive planners with costly and complex
technical problems in battle management. Soviet attempts to exhaust defenses by maintaining a superior balance of offensive forces
would be costly, and Soviet leaders would undoubtedly harbor
grave doubts about their adequacy to execute Soviet strategic doctrine. Attacks by orbital ASATs followed by saturation of a portion
of the satellite fleet that is over the target area at any given time,
however, are more feasible, and would require defensive responses
in the form of additional battle stations or technical breakthroughs
that would allow quick orbital changes and the corresponding capability to mass defensive forces. The fuel requirements and response time for orbital flexibility make this option unattractive

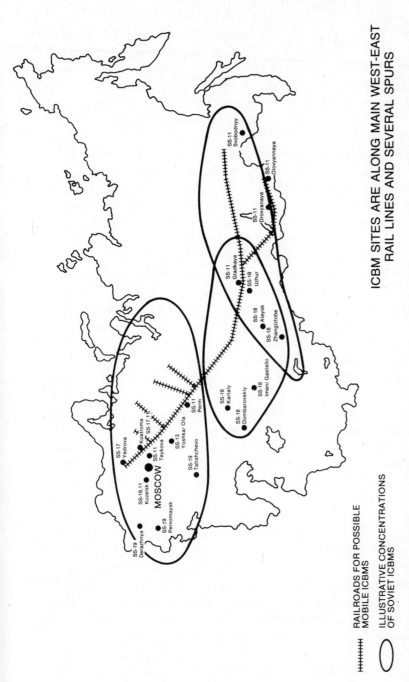

ICBM SITES ARE ALONG MAIN WEST-EAST RAIL LINES AND SEVERAL SPURS

╫╫╫╫╫ RAILROADS FOR POSSIBLE MOBILE ICBMS

◯ ILLUSTRATIVE CONCENTRATIONS OF SOVIET ICBMS

Figure 5–1. *Soviet ICBM Deployments*

Source: Derived from Robert P. Berman and John C. Baker, *Soviet Strategic Forces* (Washington, D.C.: Brookings Institution, 1982), 16–17; U.S. Department of Defense, *Soviet Military Power*, 3d ed. (Washington, D.C.: GPO, 1984), 21; and Gary L. Guertner, "Strategic Vulnerability of a Multinational State: Deterring the Soviet Union," *Political Science Quarterly* 96 (Summer 1981): 212.

from both cost and battle management perspectives. Additional battle stations could drive costs closer to the estimates of critics and further weaken political support for strategic defense. These Soviet tactical adaptations could also threaten strategic stability by rewarding the Soviet doctrinal preference for massive, preemptive attacks over the United States preference for limited attack options and escalation control.

Before strategic defense can contribute to stability, both sides must be satisfied that their offensive forces are survivable against either style of preemptive attack. A mutually constrained offense is essential to achieving this posture. Defenses combined with current trends in offensive weapons create even greater problems of instability—problems that would not exist if the defenses had not been added to the strategic relationship. Defensive inferiority in an environment of growing offensive, hard-target kill capability will be perceived as threatening by the disadvantaged party. In a crisis, striking first may seem its most rational option, because delay could result in a disarming first-strike by the side with defensive superiority. Whichever side goes first gains the damage-limiting advantage, while the side that waits may be destroyed.

It is important to remember that such terms as *damage limitation* and *rational* are relative. Prospects for either side will be horrifying, but one option could be less horrifying than another. There is a difference between wartime and peacetime concepts of rationality. Options narrow during war. There, a rational choice could be an unacceptable option if considered under peacetime conditions. The most desirable options are generally lost with the outbreak of hostilities. Planners must anticipate wartime rationality based on significantly reduced choices of action if they are to evaluate correctly the credibility of their military forces and strategies.

Crisis rationality is a point often missed by strategists, especially by many SDI enthusiasts who postulate the deterrent value of strategic defense against a Soviet "bolt out of the blue" or strategic temptation, rather than in an escalating crisis. For example, retired General Daniel O.Graham, director of High Frontier, recently made the following analogy in response to SDI critics:

> The system would have to work when needed, but if it failed, it would not fail like an alarm clock but like a minefield, and you

don't go running through a minefield simply because you think that one or two of the individual mines might not work. The mere existence of a defensive system would make the results of a missile attack so dubious that it would never be launched, and thus the system would perform its intended function: the prevention of nuclear attack.[2]

Graham's analogy is based on peacetime rationality. If we apply it to actual wartime conditions or crisis decision making, it may not accurately reflect how an adversary perceives or evaluates the range of choices actually available. Suppose, for example, that a Soviet military commander on the attack finds General Graham's minefield between his troops and sheltered positions near their objective. If he also learns that he is about to come under intense artillery attack, then he may see his options quickly narrowed to slowing his attack to clear the minefield and suffering given higher casualties from the artillery attack, or he may choose to continue attacking through the minefield while he is still at full strength.

The point is, there are wartime conditions that make poor options appear rational. The same is true if strategic stability is lost to an offensive–defensive arms race and one or both sides believes during a crisis that it is about to be attacked. Attacking first under such conditions might make sense regardless of the enemy's defenses. The choice in both examples is narrowed to attacking the same defense while at full strength or after severe attrition. By contrast, time and options can be bought with survivable offensive forces maintained through unilateral basing and deployment modes—such as mobile ICBMs and additional submarines and with formal defensive constraints. Therein lies the essence of strategic stability.

Circumvention by Bombers and Cruise Missiles

The Strategic Defense Initiative Organization has made it clear that its mandate is limited to research of a layered defense against ballistic missiles. If such a defense were deployed today, it might deter or defend against an attack by approximately 90 percent of Soviet strategic nuclear forces consisting of ICBMs and submarine-launched ballistic missiles (SLBMs). If confronted with an expanding American ballistic missile defense system, the Soviets cannot be expected to maintain this same structure. In the absence of arms control constraints, they could be expected to expand their bomber forces with a mix of long-range Bear-H and BLACKJACK bombers armed with cruise missiles. These programs are well advanced, and in some cases, in limited production. Thousands of Soviet air-launched cruise missiles could be deployed years ahead of United States ballistic missile defenses.

At sea, the Soviets could begin deploying large numbers of sea-launched cruise missiles on submarines and surface vessels. Expanded sea-based nuclear forces would confront a highly regarded American ASW capability, but risks may be manageable with the modernized Soviet navy ideally configured to protect its submarine fleet. Geographic asymmetries afforded by the long North American coastlines provide Soviet sea-based forces with lucrative targets plagued by short warning time. Combined air- and sea-based threats would drive United States air defense requirements higher than at any time since the 1950s and early 1960s. In short, a multibillion-dollar ballistic missile defense system could not only be threatened with direct assault, but also with envelopment by expanded bomber and cruise missile components of the Soviet strategic triad.

Inevitably, SDI must breed ADI (air defense initiative). Major General John Shaud, director of plans for the Air Force, anticipated these requirements in his comment, "If you are going to fix the roof, you don't want to leave the windows opened." Secretary Weinberger and others anticipate closing those "windows," and have conceded that SDI will require the backup of a restored air defense.[3]

Cost estimates vary widely for modernized ground radars, airborne warning and control system (AWACS), and interceptors to counter a growing threat from low-flying Soviet bombers and cruise missiles. Whatever their costs, the prospect of a vastly expanded and modernized air defense illustrates the inexorable logic of the offensive–defensive relationship—one threat leads to another in the absence of constraints.

Conventional Superiority in Europe

Conventional force postures may also be affected by strategic defense. If defenses succeed in limiting the threat from offensive nuclear forces, what will that success look like for NATO? Will the world be safer for conventional warfare, and if so, how might that translate into additional requirements for procurement, personnel, and conventional weapons that are needed to deter the Soviets' massive capabilities on the ground? How will the United States strategy of extended deterrence be affected if NATO's nuclear umbrella disappears in a defense-dominant world?

In addition, NATO allies could face the prospect of increased demands on their resources to deter conventional aggression in Europe during a time of growing controversy over burden sharing. An abrogated ABM Treaty could also expose them to rapid Soviet deployments of state-of-the-art ABM systems that would be effective against limited British and French nuclear deterrents currently undergoing costly modernization. In a defense-dominant world, the deterrent value of these forces would give way to the conventional balance and battlefield nuclear weapons. Short-range, low-yield, but predictably large numbers of tactical nuclear weapons would ensure the continued high cost of fielding and protecting the full spectrum of conventional forces required to fight Europe's air–land battle.

Serious doubts have also been raised over SDI's potential for boost and midcourse interception capabilities against the shorter flight times of intermediate and short-range missiles threatening Europe. These systems are most vulnerable to terminal defenses, but the large numbers of interceptors that would be required to defend against even current levels of Soviet theater nuclear forces would be costly and politically difficult to deploy in the wake of the Pershing II and ground launched cruise missile (GLCM) controversies.

Judging from European public opinion polls, the Strategic Defense Initiative has not rallied popular opposition similar in scale to the public demonstrations against the deployment of United States intermediate-range nuclear missiles. Nevertheless, the Reagan administration has conducted a massive diplomatic effort to persuade European leaders that they should support the administration's efforts to develop strategic defenses against ballistic missiles, including the intermediate-range SS-20s that the Soviets have deployed against NATO.[4]

The intense lobbying has left many U.S. allies with a potentially irreconcilable problem. Just as many of them had won the battle against public opposition to new American weapons on their soil, they are now being asked to condition that same public to the vision of a world in which strategic defenses will make ballistic missiles impotent and obsolete.

As pressure from the United States in the form of briefings, tutorials, and economic inducements to share in SDI research contracts spreads more openly into the European debate, a growing division may emerge between European and American views of how best to deter war in Europe. When this debate shifts from its current emphasis on economic issues to the more critical issues of military strategy, attention will focus on the friction between strategic defense and the offensive forces required to link United States and European security.

During the missile debate it was argued that intermediate-range nuclear weapons must be deployed in western Europe to establish credible deterrence. The potential strategic contradictions between these missiles and strategic defense can be seen best through West German eyes. The credibility of the U.S. nuclear deterrent was perceived to have been weakened by Soviet–American nuclear parity. Many West Germans feared that the Soviet Union no longer believed that the United States would retaliate in the event of a nuclear attack on Germany. The Soviet threat of escalation against the United States weakened the American nuclear umbrella over West Germany. Intermediate-range missiles based on West German soil that could reach Soviet territory, however, would reinforce deterrence by guaranteeing that nuclear war would not be isolated to Europe's central front.

The strategic coupling of American and West German security through intermediate-range missiles in the Federal Republic serves the greater German interest of strengthening deterrence. Strategic defense, on the other hand, raises many of the same concerns Germans have previously expressed over American efforts to raise the nuclear threshold through greater reliance on conventional military forces. The conventional defenses of Europe combined with credible threats to employ short-range, battlefield nuclear weapons, and to strike deep behind Soviet lines with either conventional or nuclear weapons comprises the basic United States strategy of flexible response.

As a deterrent to aggression, the emphasis on conventional defense has never been popular with West German strategists, because defending with conventional weapons increases the likelihood of carrying out a so-called "defense in depth" on West German soil that would result in large-scale devastation to territory and heavy military and civilian casualties. In the event of attack, before such reinforcements arrived, the battle could have penetrated deep into the heavily populated West German heartland where collateral damage from NATO's battlefield nuclear weapons would be highest and credible threats to employ them are lowest.

West Germans prefer to think in terms of forward defense, early use of nuclear weapons, and striking Warsaw Pact forces in their own territory with weapons that Soviet strategic defenses may make "impotent and obsolete," to borrow President Reagan's phrase. In general, West Germans understandably emphasize deterrence over war-fighting and see deterrence maintained over the long run only if there is a shared American–European community of risk. Strategic defense may reduce the threat from intercontinental and intermediate-range nuclear missiles. But defensive breakthroughs against ballistic missiles could leave Europeans with unattractive conventional options and expenditures, or a fortress America that gives rise to increased bilateralism in Soviet–United States relations. Either would risk the unraveling of the shared community of risk on which the ultimate credibility of the NATO alliance may rest.

Europeans who support SDI research do so in the context of arms control and potential bargaining leverage against Soviet offensive forces. Many Europeans have also expressed fears that their future economic role in space technology may be little more than that of a subcontractor to the American research and development juggernaut. A minor role for European industry risks loss of commercial access to new technologies and a decline in European competitiveness in world markets. These fears have increased the interest in France's "Eureka" proposal to pool European technologic resources. Joint efforts into commercially promising technology could make Europeans more competitive and far less dependent on the commercial spinoffs of United States defense-dominated research.

The European economic role in SDI, however, will not be the

decisive element in the debate. Support will eventually rise or fall on questions of military strategy. This will be especially true if Europeans become convinced that strategic defense will require greater economic burdens to support conventional defenses against a Soviet army which is much closer to them than it is to their American ally. For these reasons, European support in the absence of nuclear or conventional arms control agreements is unlikely regardless of American political pressure or technological successes.

Other problems such as the future of the NATO air defenses will inevitably place additional strains on the alliance during the SDI debate. The air defense component of a future European strategic defense posture would be far more complicated than that facing the United States. Western European air space is directly accessible to Soviet aircraft in eastern Europe, which (together with medium bombers from Soviet territory) could mount a nuclear air offensive far larger than could be mounted against North America. This asymmetry of vulnerability could easily be used to fan European sensitivities and fear that SDI will decrease the American commitment to the defense of NATO.

Conclusion

SDI may provide the transition to a safer world. The historical trends summarized here suggest, however, that even a successful transition will be only a temporary plateau in the offensive–defensive relationship. Given the many uncertainties, the burden of proof is decidedly on those who advocate proceeding, even in the absence of offensive-arms constraints. A balanced military posture must credibly deter or meet all contingencies on the spectrum of threat from low-intensity warfare to nuclear war. These needs compete in programs to deploy a six-hundred-ship navy, to modernize NATO, to deploy forces under the Central Command, and to meet the growing challenge in Central America. Investing a disproportionate share of resources in the least likely nuclear contingencies runs the risk of beggaring conventional and limited war capabilities. This, in turn, could spark conflicts that could otherwise be deterred or met decisively before they escalate to superpower confrontations.

There is a great deal at stake in the strategic defense debate.

Scientists and engineers have yet to test questions of systemic feasibility, let alone reliability. Military strategists have barely begun to consider the long-range implications of a defense-dominant world for United States global military strategy. The Congress and the American public have every right to be cautious and skeptical. Strategic defense is appealing, but it may be an illusion that could block the search for strategic stability, arms control, and a balanced military posture to meet the most probable threats to American security in the twenty-first century.

Notes

1. See, for example, *Directed Energy Missile Defense in Space—A Background Paper* (Washington, D.C.: United States Congress Office of Technology Assessment, 1984); Sidney Drell *et al.*, "Preserving the ABM Treaty: A Critique of the Reagan Strategic Defense Initiative," *International Security* 9, no. 2 (Fall 1984):67–83; Leon Sloss, "The Return of Strategic Defense," *Strategic Review* 12 (Summer 1984):37–44.
2. *New York Times*, January 18, 1985, p. A26.
3. *Washington Post*, August 25, 1984, p. A4.
4. The administration has made a major diplomatic effort to enlist European support for SDI. For a detailed study of European fears, see Paul Gallis, Mark M. Lowenthal, and Marcia Smith, *The Strategic Defense Initiative and US Alliance Strategy*, (Washington, D.C.: Congressional Research Office, 1985).

6
Offensive Doctrine in a Defense-Dominant World

It is easy to agree with proponents of strategic defense who argue that it is better to protect the American people from nuclear attack than to avenge them. There is a danger, however, that oversimplified appeals may detract from important issues of military strategy in a defense-dominant world. Deterrence can never rest on defense alone. Without offensive teeth, failure becomes the only penalty for aggression. The threat of offensive retaliation in some form will and should remain part of United States strategic doctrine. The strategic defense debate has raised serious questions about what form the offensive component of United States strategic doctrine may take in the twenty-first century.

New technology is not likely to be a substitute for offensive strategy or even for the classical theories of war. Clausewitz, for example, in his study of war which has become a standard text in the curriculum of American war colleges, devoted extensive effort to the analysis of defense. He concluded that defense was a stronger form of war than the attack. But defense was not purely passive. In his view, defense consisted of two phases: waiting for a blow and parrying it. This latter and sometimes forgotten action was intrinsic to Clausewitz's whole concept of defense. An army took up defensive positions in order to fight from them. A defense was a shield, but an active shield, one "made up of well-directed blows."[1] Clausewitz's defensive strategy consisted of finding a proper balance between offense and defense; waiting and countering; and choosing the right time and place to unleash that "flashing sword of vengeance" which he described as "the greatest moment for the defender."[2]

The SDI debate has reflected little of this kind of thinking. Rhetorical excesses have created the impression that new technologies may become so reliable that the United States will be able to sheathe its strategic sword and rely on its shield. Beating our swords into satellites will not free us from the threat of nuclear war. Offensive forces will remain in one form or another. This chapter examines these issues and the offensive–defensive relationship during the projected transition period to a defense-dominant world.

The Evolution of Strategic Offense

Classically, deterrence of war and strategic nuclear weapons employment policies have a paradoxical relationship in that deterring nuclear war has required policies and credible plans and strategies for fighting and, if not winning, at least assuring that potential adversaries could not win. While "winning" a nuclear war has little meaning in view of the major destruction that would accompany the use of nuclear weapons, it still seems clear that to be deterred, potential aggressors must be denied confidence that they could achieve their war aims.

The strategic doctrines of the United States and the Soviet Union have evolved from this paradox with important differences in emphasis.[3] United States force structure and declared employment policies have evolved to deter Soviet execution of their war plans through assured retaliation by survivable American nuclear forces. Current strategy increasingly includes "damage limitation"[4] through preferential attack options against Soviet military targets and the threat of escalation to urban and industrial targets if aggression continues. The most salient feature of this doctrine has been the evolution (described shortly) of graduated and flexible responses that incorporate limited nuclear attacks to maintain options for intrawar bargaining, escalation control, and prompt conflict termination.

Soviet doctrine places greater emphasis on war-fighting and damage limitation through large-scale, preemptive attacks against military targets. Soviet force structure and military strategy emphasize that the better their armed forces are prepared to fight a nuclear war, the better their society is equipped to survive its effects, and that the more clearly the adversary understands this, the more it will be effectively deterred. This doctrine is sometimes called "deterrence through denial"—that is, seeking to deny the opponent the prospect of military victory. It covers all of the Soviet's strategic bases since it rests on well-established war-fighting doctrines and capabilities in the event that deterrence fails. American strategists who favor war-fighting options against Soviet military targets also argue that "denial" of military victory is a far more credible strategy than threats to punish an attacker by retaliating against civilian populations.

Although Soviet and American strategic doctrines are partially converging in their emphasis on hard-target counterforce and damage-limiting capabilities, potentially destabilizing doctrinal differences remain. The most obvious is the apparent Soviet rejection of limited nuclear war concepts including escalation control and intra-war bargaining. The Soviets view these concepts as attempts at political intimidation, rather than elements in a strategy conceived by those who take war seriously. For the Soviets, denial of military victory requires robust preemption when war appears imminent, and attacks of greater magnitude than those prescribed by United States limited nuclear war strategy.

The credibility of both doctrines is sensitive to the evolving relationships between offensive and defensive forces, and is complicated by the fact that nothing in nuclear strategy is purely defensive in the sense that it does not directly support or lend credibility to offensive operations. Any calculation of a first-strike or preemption is conditioned in part by active (such as BMD) and passive (such as civil defense) defensive capabilities to absorb residual second-strike forces. Any realignment of offensive and defensive strategic capabilities as envisioned by the president's new concept of strategic defense should be carefully examined for its impact on the different offensive doctrines of the Soviet Union and United States.

A strategy incorporating strategic defense may or may not add to stability or to the evolving limited nuclear war capabilities of United States forces. Those outcomes will depend on the success and reliability of developing technologies and on the Soviet Union's willingness to negotiate offensive limitations, rather than embark on new strategic initiatives of its own.

Precisely which general combinations of negotiated offensive–defensive constraints would degrade Soviet capabilities most is debatable because of operational uncertainties. On balance, offensive reductions would affect the Soviet's robust style of preemption/damage limitation more than they would influence the evolving United States strategy of limited attack options and escalation control. Defensive constraints affect both American and Soviet strategic doctrine. When combined with offensive limits, however, they degrade the effectiveness of Soviet forces more than those of the United States, since defensive constraints make the execution of limited nuclear options more credible than a Soviet strategy based on massive preemption.

Defensive advantages by either side will greatly enhance the credibility of its strategic doctrine. Neither side is therefore likely to accede to a posture of defensive inferiority. Failing arms control remedies, the disadvantaged party will seek to reestablish its strategic position through offensive countermeasures, defensive countermeasures, or both. In the Soviet's case, these measures could also include doctrinal modifications. For example, the Soviets could seek compensation for perceived offensive shortfalls by moving toward a "softer" strategic target set, including greater emphasis on countervalue targets to compensate for the rapidly declining penetrability of their strategic forces.

Strategic Defense and Nuclear Targeting

The president has argued repeatedly that strategic defense is both militarily and morally necessary. In a White House booklet released in January 1985, he stated:

> Certainly, there should be a better way to strengthen peace and stability, a way to move away from a future that *relies so heavily on the prospect of rapid and massive nuclear retaliation* and toward greater reliance on defensive systems which threaten no one.[5] (emphasis added)

The administration's enthusiastic appeals for its Strategic Defense Initiative have, however, misrepresented current United States strategic doctrine by ignoring the past decade's doctrinal evolution away from mutual assured destruction as well as "rapid and massive nuclear retaliation." Rhetorical excesses detract from the in-depth assessments required of the proposed shift in our strategic doctrine. It is essential, therefore, to compare current offensive doctrine and future defensive objectives as accurately as possible.

The strategic defense debate finds the administration repeating many of the arguments made during the Nixon years by advocates of limited nuclear war and flexible response. They too argued that the president needed options to simple retaliation against Soviet cities, especially if Soviet reserve forces could retaliate against previously spared American cities.

Reviewing the evolution of offensive strategy and nuclear targeting options is essential to the assessment of a future defense-dominant world. For the past two decades there has been a continuous official effort to increase the range of strategic nuclear targeting options available to the president in a crisis. Options to mutual assured destruction have been developed in the documents, strategies, and force structures of every administration since 1970, including the Reagan administration. Not since the Kennedy administration has a president been confronted with a choice between no nuclear response or the massive unleashing of our strategic forces. These changes have been characterized by plans that concentrate against military targets through limited and selective attack options that, in theory, make it possible to control escalation short of attacking cities, to bargain with the Soviets during a nuclear war, and to terminate nuclear conflict at the earliest possible time.

The first official public discussions of these issues came in President Nixon's foreign policy message to Congress on February 18, 1970:

> Should a President, in the event of a nuclear attack, be left with the single option of ordering the mass destruction of enemy civilians, in the face of the certainty that it would be followed by the mass slaughter of Americans? Should the concept of assured de-

struction be narrowly defined and should it be the only measure
of our ability to deter the variety of threats we may face?[6]

A series of studies and directives followed which provided political guidance on structuring more flexible preplanned nuclear responses in the United States war plan, or SIOP (Single Integrated
Operational Plan). Secretary of Defense James Schlesinger publicly
announced the change in targeting strategy. Assured destruction and
the old policy of initiating a suicidal strike against the cities of the
other side "were no longer adequate for deterrence." He would,
therefore, implement a set of selective options against different sets
of targets on a much more limited and flexible scale.[7]

The *Nuclear Weapons Employment Policy* (NUWEP) signed by
Schlesinger in 1974 set forth the planning assumptions, attack options, targeting objectives, and damage levels needed to satisfy the
political guidelines developed by the administration. Targets were
divided into four principal groups:

Soviet nuclear forces

Soviet conventional military forces

Military and political leadership targets (such as command
posts)[8]

Economic and industrial targets (including transportation and
energy centers)[9]

The SIOP was further divided into specific categories or "packages"
of strike options that could single out or combine various target
categories within the four general groups.[10] Only two of these categories—leadership and economic targets—are associated with mutual assured destruction, and many of those targets (dams, rail junc-
tions, leadership bunkers) are located outside major population
centers. Military targets were given top priority. By adopting the
strategy of limited nuclear options, planners reasoned that escalation might be averted short of attacking target categories in major
urban–industrial centers.

The Carter administration refined the limited nuclear war strategy by deemphasizing Soviet economic targets (thus moving still further away from mutual assured destruction). It stressed the importance of survivable strategic forces and C^3 systems (communications, command, and control) required to execute a limited nuclear war.[11]

The Reagan administration produced a *Nuclear Weapons Employment and Acquisition Master Plan* which maintained the legacy of limited nuclear warfare and stressed the requirements for strategic modernization including survivable forces and communications to execute selective attack options.[12] In fact, considerable controversy during the administration's first term focused on public discussions of fighting and "winning" limited nuclear wars.

The actual conduct of nuclear war could be considerably different than declaratory policies on either side suggest. Strategic orthodoxy could easily give way to ad hoc strategies based on last-minute military and political judgments, or even based on the chaos caused by a disrupted national command authority. Escalation, collateral damage, and the delayed effects of nuclear weapons (radiation, nuclear winter, and societal disruption) could easily drive casualties to "unacceptable" levels or bring about unforeseen consequences even if cities were not directly attacked.

There are no quick technological fixes to these dilemmas posed by different deterrence strategies. The impact of strategic defense on offensive forces and targeting policies that will remain in effect for at least the remainder of this century, however, requires far more scrutiny than it has received in a debate which, thus far, has focused on public diplomacy, technical problems, and budgeting.

The New Strategic Concept

The new strategic concept links the Strategic Defense Initiative to long-range arms control proposals. Its goal is deep cuts in offensive weapons with the development of strategic defenses over a long, carefully phased transition period. During the next ten years the United States will seek a radical reduction (build-down) in offensive nuclear arms, followed by a period of mutual transition to effective nonnuclear defense forces as technology makes such options available. In a final "ultimate period," strategic defenses could make it possible to eliminate all nuclear weapons.

Ambassador Paul Nitze described the three envisioned phases in detail during testimony before the Senate Foreign Relations Committee:

The Near Term

For the near term, at least the next ten years, we will continue to base deterrence on the ultimate threat of nuclear retaliation. Today's technology provides no alternative.

That being said, we will press for radical cuts in the number and power of strategic and intermediate-range nuclear arms. . . .

The Transition Period

Should a transition be possible, arms control would play an important role. We would, for example, seek continued reductions in offensive nuclear arms.

Concurrently, we would envisage the sides beginning to test, develop, and deploy survivable and cost-effective defenses, with particular emphasis on non-nuclear defenses. *Deterrence would thus begin to rely more on a mix of offensive nuclear and defensive systems, instead of on the threat of offensive nuclear arms alone.* (emphasis added)

The transition would continue for some time, perhaps decades. . . .

The Ultimate Period

Given the right technical and political conditions, we would hope to be able to continue the reduction of all nuclear weapons down to zero.

The total elimination of nuclear weapons would be accompanied by wide-spread deployments of effective nonnuclear defenses . . .

Were we to reach the ultimate phase, deterrence would be based on the ability of the defense to deny success to a potential aggressor's attack—whether nuclear or conventional. The strategic relationship could then be characterized as one of mutual assured security.[13]

Assuming that the Soviets could be persuaded to cooperate in the transition to a defense-dominant world (a position they publicly reject), it is important not to lose sight of the continued, long-term role of offensive weapons. During the near-term phase, for example, deterrence would continue to be based on the threat of nuclear retaliation. Offensive modernization programs would continue even if arms control agreements succeed in driving down total force levels.

The transition period calls for a "mix of offensive and defensive systems" that could be maintained (and modernized) for decades. Nuclear weapons, offensive strategies, and targeting policies would be required well into the next century. It is essential, therefore, that strategic planners carefully assess the probable impacts of such strategic shifts on United States and Soviet targeting policies. Would the transition to strategic defense make us more secure or would each side alter its nuclear employment policies in such a way that cities and population centers would face even greater danger than they have in the recent past?

The Irony of Strategic Defense

If arms control agreements succeed in reducing the levels of offensive nuclear weapons, there will still remain a visible trend line in modernization and qualitative advances in the remaining forces. Maneuverable warheads, stealth technology, and cruise missiles, to name a few, will be sufficient to create doubts about the effectiveness of defenses. Similarly, technological breakthroughs in defenses will increase the uncertainties for offensive operations. Together, offensive and defensive uncertainties may precipitate targeting policies that are as threatening as any in the past. Cities and their civilian populations could again become primary targets in a nuclear war. This would be the ultimate irony of strategic defense.

Table 6–1 illustrates the relationship between current United States strategic doctrine based on limited attack options and the evolution toward a defense-dominant world. The phases are based on Nitze's descriptions. During the initial decade, assuming a cooperative adversary, offensive nuclear forces would be reduced (and

Table 6–1
The New Strategic Concept:
Impact on U.S. Strategic Doctrine

1985*———1995 Reduce Offensive Forces	1990———1995 Interim Point Defense	1995———2015 Territorial Defense	2015—"Ultimate Period"———? Near Zero Nuclear Offensive Forces
Limited Nuclear Options Remain Credible	Reduced Credibility Against: • Strategic nuclear targets • Leadership targets • Some conventional targets Most Credible Against: • Urban/Industrial • Transportation • Energy • Population	Limited Nuclear Options Not Credible	Offensive Nuclear Doctrine not Required

Offensive Remedies:
• Technological Modernization to Penetrate/Attack Defense
• Increase Offensive Forces
• Attack High Value, Soft Targets If Deterrence Fails

*Estimated Dates

modernized) to mutually agreed upon levels. Limited attack options could remain credible throughout this period.

If the United States began to deploy interim point defenses in the 1990s, such defenses would be deployed to defend strategic forces and command and control centers. Assuming that the Soviets deployed point defenses with the same priorities, a strategy of limited attack options would have significantly reduced credibility against strategic nuclear and leadership targets. Urban industrial targets would become the most vulnerable target sets during a transition stage with extensive point defenses of retaliatory forces.

As point defenses are expanded to full-scale space-based defenses which may provide reasonably credible but less than perfect territorial defense, the credibility of limited attack options is degraded against all target categories. As column 3 of table 6–1 illustrates, several offensive countermeasures are possible. Ironically, urban/industrial targets may, as table 6–2 illustrates, become the most vulnerable to attack in a less than perfect territorial defense. Offensive planning, unless all war-fighting strategies are foregone, would avoid attacks against high expenditure/low payoff military targets, especially those that are hardened and protected by "extensive" terminal defenses. A nuclear attack would admittedly come only in the most desperate of crises, but if it occurred, targeting plans would likely have focused on soft targets where a small, surviving force would have high pay-off in its destructive effects. As table 6–2 illustrates, only urban/industrial and nondispersed conventional military targets (of the four categories) meet these criteria. The probability of nuclear war may indeed decline in direct proportion to quantitative and qualitative offensive constraints, but the possibility of war will never reach zero. Its consequences, if deterrence fails, could be catastrophic due to the assumptions each side makes about the other's defenses. The irony of strategic defense is that population centers may very likely move from the bottom to the top of targeting priorities for both the United States and the Soviet Union.

Conclusion

A strategy for controlling nuclear war short of mass destruction may, as critics claim, be a false hope. But there is a world of differ-

Table 6–2
Strategic Targeting and Strategic Defense

Target Categories	Offensive Reductions and ABM Treaty in Force		Offensive Reductions and Expanded Point Defense		Offensive Reductions and Territorial Defense	
	U.S.	S.U.	U.S.	S.U.	U.S.	S.U.
I. Strategic Nuclear	LESS VULNERABLE	LESS VULNERABLE	LEAST VULNERABLE	LEAST VULNERABLE	LEAST VULNERABLE	LEAST VULNERABLE
II. Leadership	LESS VULNERABLE	LESS VULNERABLE	LESS VULNERABLE	LESS VULNERABLE	LEAST VULNERABLE	LEAST VULNERABLE
III. Conventional Military	VULNERABLE	VULNERABLE	VULNERABLE	VULNERABLE	LESS VULNERABLE	LESS VULNERABLE
IV. Urban/Industrial	VULNERABLE	VULNERABLE	MOST VULNERABLE	MOST VULNERABLE	LESS VULNERABLE	LESS VULNERABLE
-Transportation	VULNERABLE	VULNERABLE	MOST VULNERABLE	MOST VULNERABLE	LESS VULNERABLE	LESS VULNERABLE
-Energy	VULNERABLE	VULNERABLE	MOST VULNERABLE	MOST VULNERABLE	LESS VULNERABLE	LESS VULNERABLE
-Population	VULNERABLE	VULNERABLE	MOST VULNERABLE	MOST VULNERABLE	LESS VULNERABLE	LESS VULNERABLE

ence between war plans (as in the 1950s) that deliberately provide no options other than surrender or holocaust and those developed throughout the 1970s and early 1980s that attempt to mitigate the consequences of nuclear war if deterrence fails. The distinctions between mutual assured destruction and limited nuclear war have been debated for more than two decades. That debate and whatever wisdom it may have produced should not be ignored as this and subsequent administrations move toward a defense-dominant world which may not provide more security than its predecessors. If we look to the past, we see that in the 1950s nuclear war was planned on the basis of what our bombers could find—Soviet cities. In the 1990s we may plan war on the basis of what our weapons can hit—again, cities. Like the British and French with limited nuclear resources, American and Soviet planners may be driven toward countercity targeting. We will have come full circle at great expense and, in the end, succeeded in making the world safe for mutual assured destruction. If so, the impact of strategic defense on deterrence, crisis management, and offensive targeting needs to be carefully thought through now rather than in the midst of a future Soviet–American crisis.

Notes

1. Carl von Clausewitz, *On War,* ed. and trans. Michael Howard and Peter Paret (Princeton, N.J.: Princeton University Press, 1976), p. 357.
2. Discussed extensively by Michael Howard in *Clausewitz* (Oxford U.K.: Oxford University Press, 1983), pp. 23–26.
3. Studies of Soviet and United States strategic doctrine are too numerous to cite. Those that compare and contrast the Soviet and American approaches to strategic doctrine include Fritz Ermarth, "Contrasts in American and Soviet Thought," *International Security* 3 (Fall 1978), pp. 138–155; Benjamin Lambeth, *Selective Nuclear Options in American and Soviet Strategic Policy,* R-20034-DDRE (Santa Monica, Calif.: RAND Corp., 1976); and Dennis Ross, "Rethinking Soviet Strategic Policy: Inputs and Implications," *Journal of Strategic Studies,* 1 (May 1978), pp. 3–30. For the evolution of United States strategic doctrine, see Fred Kaplan, *The Wizards of Armageddon* (New York: Simon & Schuster, 1983); Leon Sloss and Marc Dean Millot, "US Nuclear Strategy in Evolution," *Strategic Review,* (Winter 1984):19–28.
4. "Damage limitation" has two distinctly different meanings. One refers to selective attacks which limit collateral damage to the enemy. A second, more

common meaning refers to (preemptive) attacks against enemy forces before they can be used against you. The latter definition is used here.

5. Ronald Reagan, *The President's Strategic Defense Initiative* (Washington, D.C.: The White House, January 1985), p. 1.

6. Richard Nixon, *US Foreign Policy in the 1970s: A New Strategy for Peace: A report to Congress of 18 February 1970* (Washington D.C.: GPO, 1970), p. 122.

7. James Schlesinger, Writers Association luncheon, DOD Public Affairs Office, January 10, 1974, pp. 5–6.

8. These could also be considered counterforce targets in their role as nuclear command and control authorities.

9. Desmond Ball, *Targeting for Strategic Deterrence,* Adelphi Paper (London: International Institute for Strategic Studies, 1983), pp. 23–24.

10. *Ibid.,* p. 24.

11. *Ibid.,* p. 23.

12. *Ibid.* The radical shift in policy can be seen by comparing the Reagan strategic modernization speech of October 2, 1981 with his star wars speech.

13. Ambassador Paul H. Nitze, statement before the Senate Foreign Relations Committee, mimeo, February 26, 1985, pp. 2–5.

7
The Future: Arms Control or Technical Follies?

As the preceding pages have attempted to demonstrate, the barriers to erecting an effective ballistic missile defense based on the technologies comprising the SDI are formidable, perhaps insurmountable. Some of the problems are technical, matters of whether given technological difficulties can be overcome, while others speak to the political and strategic desirability or undesirability of a movement toward a defensive strategic future.

The answers are not now, and in some cases may never be, entirely clear. The question of technical feasibility and systems performance, as raised in chapter 3, can only conclusively be answered in the event of an all-out launch against the United States. Tests at a lesser level will always be subject to the charge that they are not realistic.

The fact that one is dealing with possibilities and not realities makes the task of analysis all the more difficult and speculative. Advocating or opposing SDI per se is perilous business, because one may end up being for or against something quite different than reality will have it in the long run. As a matter of principle, one can argue for or against the strategic defense generally and can speculate about whether SDI's various components or its entirety are likely to materialize, but saying much more than that is premature for any but the visionary.

Having raised that cautionary note, however, an assessment of the desirability of proceeding with the defense is entirely appropriate and necessary at this point. There have always been advocates and opponents of strategic defense, and their dialogue has been stimulated (if not necessarily improved) by the SDI. Those discussions, however, have tended to not go far beyond arguing that the defense is a good (or bad) idea that is (or is not) feasible now or at some future point.

What is needed is a serious consideration of exactly how the defensive component might be incorporated into force structure, what difference such an inclusion might make on the balance of capabilities between the superpowers, how those differences affect the kinds of declaratory postures either or both sides can credibly make, and how those changes contribute to deterrence stability or instability. In other words, does a transition to the defense, based on SDI technologies or something else, make the world a better or worse place in a strategic nuclear sense.

That is not an easy question to answer, and the attempt to do so in turn must rest on at least three related judgments. The first of these is how stable or unstable the world is now, and thus how badly change needs to occur. The second, and admittedly most speculative, is how well the defense will work, since that defines how much difference it will make. The third is whether one or both sides will have the defense, and what difference that makes.

The president clearly articulated his own conviction on the first question in his March 1983 speech announcing the movement toward SDI. In his view, the move toward the strategic defensive was necessary to remove the nuclear Damoclean sword hanging over the world. Implicit in that pleading was the notion that the world could never be an entirely stable place until that sword had been effectively removed.

By making his pronouncement, the president curiously postured himself doctrinally quite close to the nuclear disarmers, although neither the Reaganites nor disarmers embraced one another. The disarmers would solve the nuclear dilemma by doing away with the weapons while the president prefers to make them obsolete. The result, however, is largely the same; nuclear weapons are removed as an effective factor in international politics generally and in American–Soviet relations specifically.

At first blush, that would seem a laudable goal. Upon closer examination, the desirability, or certainly the necessity, of moving in that direction is not entirely clear.

Negating nuclear weapons would certainly reduce the deadliness of the world in which we live by canceling out our chief mechanism for self-incineration. A world where the effects of nuclear weapons are deflected is probably preferable to one where they are removed, since there is nothing to remove the possibility of nuclear rearmament after disarmament has occurred if the political will to do so becomes compelling. The question, however, is whether that less deadly world is also less dangerous.

The latter consideration speaks to the role nuclear weapons have had on international relations in general and U.S.–U.S.S.R. relations in specific. The obvious effect has been to create the "reign of nuclear terror" (the prospect of nuclear holocaust), but has that spectre been altogether a bad thing? It is possible to argue, and it has been put forward here, that the existence of the nuclear balance, and especially the robust and deadly balance that now exists, has improved superpower relations by forcing them to relinquish direct confrontation that could devolve to nuclear war as a foreign policy goal that can be pursued. Soviet–American relations may, it can be argued, be entirely less dangerous (in terms of the likelihood of war between them) precisely because the balance of weaponry is so deadly.

This is not, of course, an orthodox interpretation, but it does raise a question about the consequences of removing the nuclear threat from the calculus. Would truly effective defenses against nuclear attack not reopen the "nonnuclear genie's bottle" and make the world once again safe for conventional war between the major powers? Self-assured that aggressive action in Europe would not likely devolve to the nuclear obliteration of the fatherland, would the Soviets be less inhibited in their designs (assuming they harbor them) against western Europe? Would a world where nuclear weapons no longer counted necessarily be a better place, as conventional thinking has had it? If it is indeed true that the central effect of nuclear weapons has been to force the superpowers to adopt nuclear war avoidance as their paramount foreign policy goal, and if the result of that determination has been to make any war between them less likely, then that is a dynamic with which one would hardly like to interfere. Rather, one would prefer actions that reinforce that dynamic situation.

What effects a movement toward an SDI-based defense would

have on the balance and its effects on international politics depend critically on how well or poorly such a system might work. Clearly, a system that is not particularly effective (for instance one that provides an imperfect defense of retaliatory forces and essentially no defense of urban areas) makes very little difference, since it does not alter the fundamental consequences of nuclear conflict. The better a system works, however, the more difference it does make.

The further one ascends the ladder of effectiveness, the more difference the defense makes to the overall balance. Especially as one approaches the theoretical point of being able to mount an invincible defense, the prospects become particularly beguiling. There are, however, distinct pitfalls that attach to this prospect.

The first of these is the question of effectiveness. As has been argued here, the burden of proof that strategic defenses can achieve levels of performance approximating perfection lies with the proponents, and it is not an easy proof to accomplish. The major reason for this, of course, is the impossibility of conducting full-scale, and thus fully realistic, tests short of the actual event of nuclear war. Perfection is a very demanding standard, and in the defense of national populations, there is an exceedingly small margin for error, given the capabilities of modern weapons of mass destruction.

Here is where the burden lies. The adherents of assured destruction make one of their most telling points when they argue that the Siren's call of BMD may be that it promises something that it cannot, in the real event, deliver. One cannot afford to plan on the basis of an SDI, or some other kind of defense that will fail, but one can also never be entirely sure how it will perform.

A second problem is what one might call the technological trap. Once again, this is a problem that has already been addressed, but it bears reiteration. It is the problem that as the technology matures and appears more and more promising, it will achieve a momentum of its own that could lead to a positive deployment decision even if other policy considerations might suggest otherwise.

Several factors could contribute to this difficulty, as they have to similar situations such as MIRV. One is that the longer one works in a technological area, the more interests become vested in it. Project scientists and managers, contractors and subcontractors, and even the Congress develop interests because of their commitments that increase as personal and economic resources are progressively invested. Given the long period of development and the probable sums that will be expended along the way, the momentum to deploy some form of SDI could be considerable by the time the technologies mature (if they do). This momentum will be particularly severe if the prospects appear especially promising in a performance sense.

In turn, the technological trap could produce a kind of blinder's effect where an SDI decision is made in isolation from other strategic and political concerns. Here, the danger is that the United States might decide to deploy simply because it has the physical capability to do so, or because it feels that it might gain some advantage over the Soviets by exploiting a technological advantage. That was the kind of logic that largely underlay the MIRV testing decision in 1968, and the analogy is appropriate. MIRV was deployed because it represented a technological advantage that could be exploited relatively cheaply and that we did not believe the Soviets could replicate very quickly. The result, at the time foreseen by only a few whose voices were not heeded, was the MIRV race that has produced a Soviet numerical advantage and a strategic situation where our security is detracted from and not enhanced.

The third problem, which relates closely to the second, is that we will be so enamoured of the defensive prospect as to ignore the contribution of other dynamics to the arms balance, most notably the influence of arms control processes. One might call this phenomenon systemic myopia, referring to the inability to anticipate the effects of a unilateral positive deployment decision's effects on other system dynamics.

This is, once again, a familiar problem, and in this case one with a current deterrent. The analogy with MIRV once again holds. The evidence suggests that the MIRV decision was made on a narrow, largely technical and bureaucratic basis.[1] From a broader perspective, it was clear that the long-term effect of MIRV would be to create warhead proliferation and the vulnerability of offensive forces. Some saw this at the time, but they were voices in the dark whose counsel went unheeded in the glow of technical achievement.

There is a parallel here with the effects a positive SDI decision could have on arms control prospects. The Geneva arms control talks have established a broad agenda that encompasses both intermediate and strategic offensive nuclear weapons and the SDI (or strategic defenses more generically, although public attention has been focused on the SDI technologies by Soviet General Secretary Gorbachev). The question is how those different components of the strategic mix will be considered vis-a-vis one another.

These are clearly complex considerations from which many other concerns cascade, and all of them could be affected by decisions one way or the other about the SDI. A major point to be made is that serious consideration of exactly what the ramifications are has not been seriously undertaken. Unless those concerns are thoroughly analyzed and rationalized before any kinds of decisions about the SDI are made, the result could be a large number of unforeseen consequences that make matters worse rather than better. Until these problems are solved, any action on SDI must proceed with considerable caution.

There is another aspect of the arms controller's concern with systemic myopia. That is the danger that a unilateral decision to go forward with the SDI will result in an offense–defense arms race that will simply up the strategic ante with great additional costs and result in no more secure a world than that which it replaces. Unconstrained by any arms control regime, the obvious responses to SDI deployment are increased offensive forces capable of overcoming any defense, offensive capabilities aimed at destroying or neutralizing the defenses, or a reemphasis on offensive capabilities such as bombers and cruise missiles against which the SDI defenses may prove irrelevant. The result could be enormously costly, as in the case of an American need to reestablish meaningful air defenses against the Soviets, or heightened uncertainty about the relative effectiveness of offenses against defenses. In either case, one can scarcely argue that the result would be better than the current situation.

There is a final consideration about whether the addition of strategic defenses will make the world a better or worse place. That is the question of who will have them, and there are two possibilities in addition to the current situation of defenselessness. The first is that both sides will have systems of like or different capability. The second is that one side but not the other will be able to field defenses based on the SDI or some other technologies.

The most promising situation, as argued in chapter 2, is where the United States and the U.S.S.R. are able to field systems of relatively similar capability. In this circumstance, neither side would necessarily feel advantage during the transition, and the net result would be a relatively symmetrical situation.

The unresolved question is whether this most optimistic scenario would result in a world preferable to the one in which we now exist. The answer, at least from the vantage point of American thought on the subject, is not crystal clear. If one looks at the sweep of thought about deterrence, force planning, and employment strategy, American strategies have been absolutely dominated by the apparently immutable ascendancy of the offense over the defense. There is very little in the corpus of deterrence thought that makes allowance for a defensive component.

This suggests the need for a concerted endeavor to find out whether we want a defense if we can have one. Such an examination should have two foci. First, a concerted effort needs to be made well in advance of any deployment decisions to determine if strategic defense and strategic stability are compatible. If the major burden of the enterprise of deterrence is to avoid the initiation of nuclear war, and keeping incentives at a minimum is the definition of stability, then we must ask if the defense does or can contribute to that end. Assuming the first question can be answered positively, the second imperative is to prepare strategy and doctrine for the inclusion of defenses as they come on line.

If one can arguably make a case for defenses provided both sides deploy like systems (so that, for example, the problem of proliferation would be less severe), it is not so clear that the same is true if, for instance, the United States can deploy an effective defense based in the SDI while the Soviets can deploy either no defense or only one markedly inferior in capability. This possibility creates two potential problems.

On the one hand, there is the problem of transition to such a circumstance, as argued in chapter 2. The difficulty during the transitional stage is the dilemma of "use them or leave them useless" and could induce instability. On the other hand, a successful deployment for which there were no counterpart would leave the nonpossessor subject to nuclear blackmail, a circumstance neither superpower relishes.

There is some evidence to suggest one of these latter prospects may be realistic. During the 1984 election campaign President Reagan admitted the dangers of a world where one side possessed these weapons and the other did not when he proposed the possibility of sharing the technology with the Soviets. The idea, despite whatever theoretical merit it may have possessed, quickly disappeared in objections to sharing such sensitive secrets with the adversary at whom they are aimed.

The other reason for suggesting this as a reasonable possibility is the stridency of Soviet opposition to it. The Soviet assault on SDI, led by Gorbachev, may be motivated by the feeling of need to kill a project with which the Soviets feel they cannot compete. It may well be that the analogy with the period surrounding the ABM Treaty is appropriate. In that setting, the Soviets apparently used the restrictiveness of the agreement to inhibit an area of U.S. advantage; this may well be the basis of SDI oppositon as well.

As has been argued throughout these pages, any definitive judgment on the SDI is premature. The technological questions of what SDI-based defenses will and will not be able to do have not been answered, and may not be for another decade or more. At the same time, many of the strategic and policy questions about the desirability of transforming the strategic balance into one incorporating the defense remain unresolved.

SDI is, however, both an element in the domestic defense debate and a prominent arms control agenda item. Of the two, its placement in the domestic debate is the less urgent, because the central concern is only over the levels of funding (if any) to devote it. SDI will only become critical domestically when decisions to devote substantial resources to deployment become necessary.

The role of SDI on the arms control agenda is urgent. If the administration's contention is correct, it was, after all, the prospect of SDI which brought the Soviets back to the negotiating table, and the temporal sequence of events since March 1983 certainly does not contradict that interpretation. At the same time, Soviet insistence on squelching SDI and their threat to subvert the Geneva talks if this does not occur represent the clearest dangers to the ongoing process.

Where does this leave SDI?

Developing, testing, and deploying a defensive system that matches the technical specifications and performance criteria established by the Reagan administration will require Herculean efforts.

Success or even limited progress will be justifiably accompanied by a heady sense of pride and accomplishment. There is a potential danger, however, even in success if the SDI debate becomes too narrowly focused on technical breakthroughs.

Technical successes may cloud judgments on nontechnical problems at a time when decisions are required to move from research and development to deployment. In evaluating the results of research, and in making any such decisions, the Reagan and subsequent administrations will need to ask some basic questions about the future nature of United States strategy. In particular, they will have to consider how best to enhance deterrence, and how best to curb rather than stimulate a new arms race. At that stage, the judgments to be made will only partly depend upon technical assessments about the feasibility of defenses. Even if the research shows promise, the case for proceeding will have to be weighed in the light of the wider strategic implications discussed in these pages.

But can we afford even now simply to wait for the scientists and military experts to deliver their results at some later stage? Have we a breathing space of five, ten, or fifteen years before we need to address strategic concerns? The history of weapons development and the strategic balance shows only too clearly that research into new weapons and study of their strategic implications must go hand in hand. Otherwise, research may acquire a nonstoppable momentum of its own, even though the case for stopping may strengthen with the passage of years. Policy makers must take care that political decisions are not preempted by the march of technology, or by premature attempts to predict the final destination of that march.

Above all else, the transition to the defense-dominant world envisioned by the Reagan administration requires not only the continuation, but also the expansion of an arms control regime. None of the criteria for strategic defense can be met without negotiated reductions in Soviet offensive forces. This is a vital first step even if it comes at the cost of severe constraints in SDI development and testing programs.

In the short term, agreements at START and Intermediate Nuclear Forces (INF) should be a first priority. If its negotiators are successful, the United States can, over time, consolidate the newly negotiated political and military postures that will result from a future treaty, and continue both SDI research and long-range efforts to bring the Soviets into a cooperative transition to defense. A post-START–INF treaty political climate will be far more hospitable to such a transition. If "radical" reductions in offensive forces are initiated, and a phased build-down results, a major obstacle to strategic defense may be overcome—Soviet fears that the Reagan SDI is not intended to keep the Soviets from threatening (that is, deterring) the United States, but instead is intended to make sure American offensive forces can threaten them. The shield strengthens the sword; until swords are formally limited in their capabilities, the Soviets will have little incentive to negotiate defenses beyond the scope allowed by the ABM Treaty.

Many pro-arms controllers favor using SDI as a bargaining chip to trade against Soviet offensive forces. This faction views offensive reductions as an end in itself; an end which makes strategic defense irrelevant or redundant. Offensive reductions, however, can also be the crucial first step in the transition to a nonnuclear strategic defense. Radical reductions over time, combined with offensive force modernization programs that insure mutual survivability of offensive forces from a first strike could eliminate at least two of the most serious concerns expressed by arms controllers about strategic defense.

First, fears of technical reliability and effectiveness could be substantially reduced in a strategic posture of limited offensive weapons and cooperatively expanded defenses. In such an environment, defenses may be militarily effective in complicating and deterring attacks, even if they cannot claim 100 percent technical effectiveness.

Second, traditional and justifiable fears that defenses are destabilizing could give way to acceptance of deterrence resting on defense-dominated equilibrium provided: (1) offensive reductions result in mutually survivable offensive forces, and (2) philosophical shifts by arms controllers are matched by equal constraints on strategic counterforce planning and capabilities as part of any future offensive build-down.

An additional reason for moving away from doctrines of deterrence based on offensive force characteristics can be seen in the complications confronting Soviet military planners and arms controllers who must account for Chinese, British, and French nuclear forces in their bilateral arms agreements negotiated with the United States. As the number of nuclear-capable nations increases, the United States will confront similar problems in its strategic planning against multilateral threats. A Soviet–United States relationship based on strategic defense could minimize the disruption and instability often associated with nuclear proliferation.

Other problems confronting strategic planners will remain and must be evaluated against the advantages of a defense-dominant world. For example, the arms controllers' concern about costs will remain even in a successful offensive arms control regime. Costs may be driven as much by doubts about systems' reliability as by Soviet countermeasures. Ballistic missile defenses cannot be fully tested, and flaws in weapons or battle management are likely to remain undetected until real attacks make them visible. Imperfect systems can contribute to deterrence, but prudent planners will constantly push for improvements and greater reliability.

The potential offensive use of space-based defenses is also a legitimate long-range concern. Technology may create dual purpose systems that straddle both offensive and defensive missions. Orbiting battle stations may develop the capability to attack land and sea-based targets. ASATs can attack these same battle stations, and one can easily construct a scenario in which war begins with "defensive" weapons on the attack and "offensive" weapons rush to the defense.

For these and other reasons described at length in this book, the movement toward a defense-dominant world must be slow and deliberate in its efforts to meet the performance and arms control criteria evolving in the Reagan administration. The proponents of SDI must avoid what Freeman Dyson has described as the "technical-follies future."[2] The technical-follies is the open-ended offensive–defensive arms race that surely will be precipitated by unilateralists who advocate deployment of strategic defenses even in the absence of arms control. The unilateralists who would attempt to create a security regime based solely on technology could never be at rest. Soviet responses would, sooner or later, negate the best efforts of those who abandon diplomacy in their search for security. The unilateralist is both guided and blinded by the light at the front of the tunnel. Behind the light of futuristic weapons and the goal of a "perfect" defense is a strategic black hole into which the United States and the Soviet Union will almost certainly fall as the result of an open-ended and unconstrained arms competition. Technological dependency is not the foundation on which future American security should be built. Science, arms control, and military strategy must succeed together, or SDI risks becoming America's technological Vietnam.

Notes

1. Graham T. Allison, "Questions about the Arms Race: Who's Racing Whom? A Bureaucratic Perspective" in *American Defense Policy*, 4th ed., ed. John E. Endicott and Roy W. Stafford (Baltimore: Johns Hopkins University Press, 1977), pp. 424–41.
2. Freeman Dyson, *Weapons and Hope,* (New York: Harper & Row, 1984); chaps. 5, 7.

Appendix A

Concept Definitions
and Constraints

Concept Definitions
and Constraints

A Narrative Summary of Major
Administration Documents and
Testimonies on the Strategic Defense
Initiative

I n his March 23, 1983 speech, the president directed the military, scientific, and industrial communities to undertake a long-term research program to "achieve our ultimate goal of eliminating the threat posed by strategic nuclear missiles."

The president's speech was followed by NSDD-85 (March 25, 1983) and NSSD 6-83 (April 18, 1983). These documents directed two studies—one to assess the role defensive system deployments could play in future security strategy, and the second to define a research and development program aimed at an ultimate goal of eliminating the threat posed by nuclear ballistic missiles. The Future Security Strategy study, *Ballistic Missile Defenses and US National Defense (Hoffman Study),* was specifically tasked to develop criteria for preserving stable deterrence based on increasing reliance on defensive systems and decreasing reliance on offensive weapons.

The Defensive Technologies Study (Fletcher Panel) was tasked to identify the most promising directions for future scientific/technical progress to underwrite military potential. Effectiveness and not potential for early deployment was stressed as the most important criterion.

Concept Definitions

The *Defensive Technologies Study (Fletcher Panel)* took an optimistic view of newly emerging technologies and with this viewpoint concluded that a robust, multitiered BMD system could eventually be made to work. The study concluded that the ultimate utility, effectiveness, cost, complexity, and degree of technical risk in this system will depend not only on the technology itself, but also on the extent to which the Soviet Union either agrees to mutual defense arrangements and offense limitations or embarks on new strategic directions in response to our initiative. The outcome of initiating an evolutionary shift in our strategic direction will hinge on policy and technological issues that as yet are unresolved.

The panel urged that a vigorous research and development program, broadly based but highly goal oriented, be pursued. This program will permit informed decisions on whether to initiate, in the early 1990s, an engineering validation phase leading to a deployed defensive capability after the year 2000. Certain intermediate technologies can and should be demonstrated as part of the evolutionary R&D program. The panel further noted that the potential exists for earlier, phased deployment against constrained threats. The panel's report implicitly required the continuation of an arms regime to meet cost and technical requirements for ballistic missile defense.

The *Ballistic Missile Defenses and U.S. National Security Study* (Hoffman) concluded:

> Deployment of defensive systems can increase stability, but to attain this we must design our offensive and defensive forces properly—and, especially, we must not allow them to be vulnerable. In combination with other measures, defenses can contribute to reducing the prelaunch vulnerability of our offensive forces. To increase stability, defenses must themselves avoid high vulnerability, must be robust in the face of the enemy technical or tactical countermeasures, and must compete favorably in cost terms with expansion of the Soviet offensive force. A defense that was highly effective for an attack below some threshold but lost effectiveness very rapidly for larger attacks might decrease stability if superimposed on vulnerable offensive systems. Boost-phase and mid-

course layers may present problems of both vulnerability and high sensitivity to attack size. Nevertheless, if this vulnerability can be limited through technical and tactical measures, these layers may constitute very useful elements of properly designed multilayered systems where their sensitivity is compensated by the capabilities of other system components.

The Hoffman Study was less explicit than the Fletcher Panel in requiring the continuation of an arms control regime in some form. Instead, it referred to the defense competing "favorably" in cost terms with expanding Soviet offensive forces and technical and tactical measures to reduce systems vulnerability.

The Strategic Defense Initiative Organization Charter

In creating the SDIO in *DOD* Directive April 24, 1984, the secretary of defense directed that the Strategic Defense Initiative Program:

Follow the technology plan identified by the *Fletcher Panel* and the policy approach outlined in the *Hoffman Study*,

Be carried out with full consultation with our allies,

Place principal emphasis on nonnuclear technologies (Research on other concepts is to provide contingency options.),

Have for its basic approach a layered defense system that can be deployed in such a way as to increase the contribution of defenses to deterrence,

Protect United States options for near-term deployments of limited ballistic missile defenses.

Criteria for Transition to Strategic Defense

The administration has repeatedly stressed that SDI is a research program consistent with United States treaty obligations, not a program to deploy weapons:

The Strategic Defense Initiative is designed to answer a number of fundamental scientific and engineering questions that must be addressed before the promise of these new technologies can be fully assessed. It is a research program, not a program to deploy weapons. The question of whether to proceed with deployment of an actual ballistic missile defense system would arise in the years to come after the SDI research has generated the technology for effective defenses that are achievable and affordable. (Testimony by Lt. General James Abrahamson before the Senate Committee on Armed Services, February 21, 1985, p. 2)

Since the President's speech in 1983, many have attempted to interpret what his vision entailed and what the SDI was expected to accomplish. Contrary to conflicting reports, the goal has not changed but has, in fact, remained consistent with the direction outlined by the President. The driving force behind his concept is freeing the world from the fear of nuclear conflict. It should be stressed that the SDI is a *research program* that seeks to provide the technical knowledge required to support a decision on whether to develop and later deploy advanced defensive systems. It is not a program to deploy those systems. All research efforts will be fully compliant with U.S treaty obligations. (United States Department of Defense, *Report to Congress on the Strategic Defense Initiative,* 1985, p. 7)

As directed by the President, the SDI research program will be conducted in a manner fully consistent with all U.S. treaty obligations, including the 1972 ABM Treaty. The ABM Treaty prohibits the development, testing, and deployment of ABM systems and components that are space-based, air-based, sea-based, or mobile land-based. However, as Ambassador Gerard Smith, chief U.S. negotiator of the ABM Treaty, reported to the Senate Armed Services Committee in 1972, that agreement does permit research short of field testing of a prototype ABM system or component. This is the type of research that will be conducted under the SDI program. (*Ibid.*, p. 8, and *The President's Strategic Defense Initiative,* White House booklet, January 1985, p. 5)

A decision to deploy a strategic defense system will depend on achieving the following technical capabilities and cost criteria:

1. Technologies must be achievable (technologically reliable).
2. Systems must be effective (lethal against Soviet offensive forces).
3. Systems must be affordable.
4. Defense must be cost-effective at the margin. (Deploying additional increments of defense is cheaper than deploying additional offensive countermeasures.)
5. Systems must be survivable.
6. Strategic defense must enhance deterrence.

Administration statements on these criteria include:

> If the SDI is to offer a high confidence basis for decisions to pursue one or more defensive options, the research program must do several things. . . . It must identify and evaluate the potential effectiveness of candidate ballistic missile defenses that could be assembled and deployed from those technologies. It must provide a basis for showing how those defense options can be operated and maintained to do the job.
>
> To achieve the major SDI goal, the SDIO must bring along the emerging technologies in a logical, timely way in this, the initial stage of the SDI. . . . The most mature technologies need to be validated to provide initial options based on defense architectures that are affordable, survivable, and effective. (*DOD Report to Congress on the Strategic Defense Initiative*, 1985, p. 9)

> To achieve the benefits which advanced defensive technologies could offer, they must, at a minimum, be able to destroy a sufficient portion of an aggressor's attacking forces to deny him confidence in the outcome of an attack or deny an aggressor the ability to destroy a militarily significant portion of the target base he wishes to attack. Any effective defensive system must, of course, be survivable and cost-effective.
>
> To achieve the required level of survivability, the defensive system need not be invulnerable, but must be able to maintain a sufficient degree of effectiveness to fulfill its mission, even in the face of determined attacks against it. This characteristic is essential not only to maintain the effectiveness of a defense system, but to maintain stability.

Finally, in the interest of discouraging the proliferation of ballistic missile forces, the defensive system must be able to maintain its effectiveness against the offense at less cost than it would take to develop offensive countermeasures and proliferate the ballistic missiles necessary to overcome it. (*The President's Strategic Defense Initiative,* White House booklet, January 1985, p. 5)

To achieve our major goal, we must bring along the emerging technologies in a logical, timely way. The overall research task is expected to bring the technologies to maturity in three developmental thrusts. First, we need to validate the most mature technologies to provide the opportunity for our national leadership to decide whether to pursue initial defense options based on those technologies that are affordable, survivable, and effective. They could decide on an initial step which implements a defense against the threat we believe will be in place at least until early in the next century or they could decide to reserve the options as a simple hedge against Soviet breakout and development of a defense against U.S. ballistic missiles. Second, we need to ensure the long-term viability of future defensive options by demonstrating by the early 1990s, the feasibility and readiness of technologies to support the validation of more advanced defense options. And third, we need to conduct research that encourages the innovation of the U.S. scientific community in a response to the President's challenge to aid SDI research in identifying new approaches for eliminating the threat of ballistic misssiles. (Arms Control Impact Statement, FY 1986, Washington, D.C.: U.S. Arms Control and Disarmament Agency, April 1985, p. 8.)

In pursuing defense-in-depth options, a broad range of technologies must be developed in order to perform the five basic functions of any defense:

Detection of the threat and alerting the defense elements;

Acquisition and tracking of the threat to locate it in time and space;

Identification of the threat and discrimination against decoys to insure efficient allocation of the defense resources;

Interception and destruction of the threat; and

Assessment of the results of the engagement.

These five functions are performed repeatedly in the separate engagements of the ballistic missiles in their four phases of flight (boost, post-boost, midcourse, and terminal). (Statement on the Strategic Defense Initative by Lt. General James A. Abrahamson before the Committee on Armed Services, United States Senate, February 21, 1985, pp. 6, 8.)

To maintain stability after deployment, defensive systems would have to be cost effective relative to ballistic missiles in order to avoid creating incentives for the proliferation of offensive forces. To the extent that significant negotiated ballistic missile reductions could be achieved, such reductions in turn would serve to increase the effectiveness and deterrent potential of defensive systems. A basic question for stability will be the difference between the marginal costs of additional offensive weapons with improved delivery capability, and the marginal costs or responsive increments to defensive systems. (Arms Control Impact Statement FY 1986, Washington, D.C.: U.S. Arms Control and Disarmament Agency, April 1985, p. 8.)

I should note that the criteria by which we will judge the feasibility of new defensive technologies will be demanding. The technologies must produce defensive systems that are reasonably survivable; if not, the defense would themselves be tempting targets for a first strike. This would decrease, rather than enhance, stability.

Moreover, new defenses should be cost-effective at the margin, that is, effective enough and cheap enough to add additional defensive capability so that the other side has no incentive to add additional offensive capability to overcome the defense. Otherwise, the defensive systems could, if not restrained by mutual agreement, encourage a proliferation of countermeasures and offensive weapons to overcome deployed defenses, instead of a redirection of effort from offense to defense.

If new technologies cannot meet these standards, we would

not deploy them. We would then continue to base deterrence on the ultimate threat of nuclear retaliation. (Statement by Ambassador Paul H. Nitze before the Senate Foreign Relations Committee, February 26, 1985, p. 3).

The New Strategic Concept: Managing the Transition to Strategic Defense

Beginning with the Shultz–Gromyko meeting in January 1985, and continuing into the current negotiations, the United States has made it clear that its objectives go beyond negotiated reductions in offensive nuclear weapons. The Geneva negotiations are a forum where the administration is addressing the means for enhancing stability and reducing the risk of war through mutual transition to strategic defense. The "new strategic concept" was first summarized publicly in a speech by Deputy Secretary of State Kenneth Dam (*Current Policy* No. 647, United States Department of State, January 14,1985) and later by Ambassador Paul Nitze during testimony before the Senate Foreign Relations Committee on February 26, 1985:

> During the next ten years, the U.S. objective is a radical reduction in the power of existing and planned offensive nuclear arms, as well as the stabilization of the relationship between offensive and defensive nuclear arms, whether on earth or in space. We are even now looking forward to a period of transition to a more stable world, with greatly reduced levels of nuclear arms and an enhanced ability to deter war based upon an increasing contribution of non-nuclear defenses against offensive nuclear arms. This period of transition could lead to the eventual elimination of all nuclear arms, both offensive and defensive. A world free of nuclear arms is an ultimate objective to which we, the Soviet Union, and all other nations can agree.

This concept details three time phases: the near term, a transition phase, and an ultimate phase.

The Near Term

For the near term, at least the next ten years, we will continue to base deterrence on the ultimate threat of nuclear retaliation. Today's technology provides no alternative. . . .

That being said, we will press for radical cuts in the number and power of strategic and intermediate-range nuclear arms. . . .

The Transition Period

Should a transition be possible, arms control would play an important role. We would, for example, seek continued reductions in offensive nuclear arms. . . .

Concurrently, we would envisage the sides beginning to test, develop, and deploy survivable and cost-effective defenses, with particular emphasis on non-nuclear defenses. Deterrence would thus begin to rely more on a mix of offensive nuclear and defensive systems, instead of on the threat of offensive nuclear arms alone. . . .

The transition would continue for some time, perhaps decades. . . .

"The Ultimate Period"

Given the right technical and political conditions, we would hope to be able to continue the reduction of all nuclear weapons down to zero. . . .

The total elimination of nuclear weapons would be accompanied by wide-spread deployments of effective non-nuclear defenses. . . .

Were we to reach the ultimate phase, deterrence would be based on the ability of the defense to deny success to a potential aggressor's attack—whether nuclear or conventional. The strategic relationship could then be characterized as one of mutual assured security. . . .

Appendix B

ABM Treaty and Associated Documents

Reprinted from *Arms Control and Disarmament Agreements: Texts and Histories of Agreements* (Washington, D.C.: United States Arms Control and Disarmament Agency, 1982), pp. 139–147; 161.

Treaty Between the United States of America and the Union of Soviet Socialist Republics on the Limitation of Anti-Ballistic Missile Systems

Signed at Moscow May 26, 1972
Ratification advised by U.S. Senate August 3, 1972
Ratified by U.S. President September 30, 1972
Proclaimed by U.S. President October 3, 1972
Instruments of ratification exchanged October 3, 1972
Entered into force October 3, 1972

The United States of America and the Union of Soviet Socialist Republics, hereinafter referred to as the Parties,

Proceeding from the premise that nuclear war would have devastating consequences for all mankind,

Considering that effective measures to limit anti-ballistic missile systems would be a substantial factor in curbing the race in strategic offensive arms and would lead to a decrease in the risk of outbreak of war involving nuclear weapons,

Proceeding from the premise that the limitation of anti-ballistic missile systems, as well as certain agreed measures with respect to the limitation of strategic offensive arms, would contribute to the creation of more favorable conditions for further negotiations on limiting strategic arms,

Mindful of their obligations under Article VI of the Treaty on the Non-Proliferation of Nuclear Weapons,

Declaring their intention to achieve at the earliest possible date the cessation of the nuclear arms race and to take effective measures toward reductions in strategic arms, nuclear disarmament, and general and complete disarmament,

Desiring to contribute to the relaxation of international tension and the strengthening of trust between States,

Have agreed as follows:

Article I

1. Each party undertakes to limit anti-ballistic missile (ABM) systems and to adopt other measures in accordance with the provisions of this Treaty.

2. Each Party undertakes not to deploy ABM systems for a defense of the territory of its country and not to provide a base for such a defense, and not to deploy ABM systems for defense of an individual region except as provided for in Article III of this Treaty.

Article II

1. For the purpose of this Treaty an ABM system is a system to counter strategic ballistic missiles or their elements in flight trajectory, currently consisting of:

(a) ABM interceptor missiles, which are interceptor missiles constructed and deployed for an ABM role, or of a type tested in an ABM mode;

(b) ABM launchers, which are launchers constructed and deployed for launching ABM interceptor missiles; and

(c) ABM radars, which are radars constructed and deployed for an ABM role, or of a type tested in an ABM mode.

2. The ABM system components listed in paragraph 1 of this Article include those which are:

(a) operational;
(b) under construction;
(c) undergoing testing;
(d) undergoing overhaul, repair or conversion; or
(e) mothballed.

Article III

Each Party undertakes not to deploy ABM systems or their components except that:

(a) within one ABM system deployment area having a radius of one hundred and fifty kilometers and centered on the Party's national capital, a Party may deploy: (1) no more than one hundred ABM launchers and no more than one hundred ABM interceptor missiles at launch sites, and (2) ABM radars within no more than six ABM radar complexes, the area of each complex being circular and having a diameter of no more than three kilometers; and

(b) within one ABM system deployment area having a radius of one hundred and fifty kilometers and containing ICBM silo launchers, a Party may deploy: (1) no more than one hundred ABM launchers and no more than one hundred ABM interceptor missiles at launch sites, (2) two large phased-array ABM radars comparable in potential to corresponding ABM radars operational or under construction on the date of signature of the Treaty in an ABM system deployment area containing ICBM silo launchers, and (3) no more than eighteen ABM radars each having a potential less than the potential of the smaller of the above-mentioned two large phased-array ABM radars.

Article IV

The limitations provided for in Article III shall not apply to ABM systems or their components used for development or testing, and located within current or additionally agreed test ranges. Each Party may have no more than a total of fifteen ABM launchers at test ranges.

Article V

1. Each Party undertakes not to develop, test, or deploy ABM systems or components which are sea-based, air-based, space-based, or mobile land-based.

2. Each Party undertakes not to develop, test, or deploy ABM launchers for launching more than one ABM interceptor missile at a time from each launcher, not to modify deployed launchers to provide them with such a capability, not to develop, test, or deploy automatic or semi-automatic or other similar systems for rapid reload of ABM launchers.

Article VI

To enhance assurance of the effectiveness of the limitations on ABM systems and their components provided by the Treaty, each Party undertakes:

(a) not to give missiles, launchers, or radars, other than ABM interceptor missiles, ABM launchers, or ABM radars, capabilities to counter strategic ballistic missiles or their elements in flight trajectory, and not to test them in an ABM mode; and

(b) not to deploy in the future radars for early warning of strategic ballistic missile attack except at locations along the periphery of its national territory and oriented outward.

Article VII

Subject to the provisions of this Treaty, modernization and replacement of ABM systems or their components may be carried out.

Article VIII

ABM systems or their components in excess of the numbers or outside the areas specified in this Treaty, as well as ABM systems or their components prohibited by this Treaty, shall be destroyed or dismantled under agreed procedures within the shortest possible agreed period of time.

Article IX

To assure the viability and effectiveness of this Treaty, each Party undertakes not to transfer to other States, and not to deploy outside its national territory, ABM systems or their components limited by this Treaty.

Article X

Each Party undertakes not to assume any international obligations which would conflict with this Treaty.

Article XI

The Parties undertake to continue active negotiations for limitations on strategic offensive arms.

Article XII

1. For the purpose of providing assurance of compliance with the provisions of this Treaty, each Party shall use national technical means of verification at its disposal in a manner consistent with generally recognized principles of international law.

2. Each Party undertakes not to interfere with the national technical means of verification of the other Party operating in accordance with paragraph 1 of this Article.

3. Each Party undertakes not to use deliberate concealment measures which impede verification by national technical means of compliance with the provisions of this Treaty. This obligation shall not require changes in current construction, assembly, conversion, or overhaul practices.

Article XIII

1. To promote the objectives and implementation of the provisions of this Treaty, the Parties shall establish promptly a Standing Consultative Commission, within the framework of which they will:

(a) consider questions concerning compliance with the obligations assumed and related situations which may be considered ambiguous;

(b) provide on a voluntary basis such information as either Party considers necessary to assure confidence in compliance with the obligations assumed;

(c) consider questions involving unintended interference with national technical means of verification;

(d) consider possible changes in the strategic situation which have a bearing on the provisions of this Treaty;

(e) agree upon procedures and dates for destruction or dismantling of ABM systems or their components in cases provided for by the provisions of this Treaty;

(f) consider, as appropriate, possible proposals for further increasing the viability of this Treaty; including proposals for amendments in accordance with the provisions of this Treaty;

(g) consider, as appropriate, proposals for further measures aimed at limiting strategic arms.

2. The Parties through consultation shall establish, and may amend as appropriate, Regulations for the Standing Consultative Commission governing procedures, composition and other relevant matters.

Article XIV

1. Each Party may propose amendments to this Treaty. Agreed amendments shall enter into force in accordance with the procedures governing the entry into force of this Treaty.

2. Five years after entry into force of this Treaty, and at five-year intervals thereafter, the Parties shall together conduct a review of this Treaty.

Article XV

1. This Treaty shall be of unlimited duration.

2. Each Party shall, in exercising its national sovereignty, have the right to withdraw from this Treaty if it decides that extraordinary events related to the subject matter of this Treaty have jeopardized its supreme interests. It shall give notice of its decision to the other Party six months prior to withdrawal from the Treaty. Such notice shall include a statement of the extraordinary events the notifying Party regards as having jeopardized its supreme interests.

Article XVI

1. This Treaty shall be subject to ratification in accordance with the constitutional procedures of each Party. The Treaty shall enter into force on the day of the exchange of instruments of ratification.

2. This Treaty shall be registered pursuant to Article 102 of the Charter of the United Nations.

DONE at Moscow on May 26, 1972, in two copies, each in the English and Russian languages, both texts being equally authentic.

FOR THE UNITED STATES OF AMERICA

FOR THE UNION OF SOVIET SOCIALIST REPUBLICS

RICHARD NIXON

L. I. BREZHNEV

President of the United States of America

General Secretary of the Central Committee of the CPSU

Agreed Statements, Common Understandings, and Unilateral Statements Regarding the Treaty Between the United States of America and the Union of Soviet Socialist Republics on the Limitation of Anti-Ballistic Missiles

1. Agreed Statements

The document set forth below was agreed upon and initialed by the Heads of the Delegations on May 26, 1972 (letter designations added);

AGREED STATEMENTS REGARDING THE TREATY BETWEEN THE UNITED STATES OF AMERICA AND THE UNION OF SOVIET SOCIALIST REPUBLICS ON THE LIMITATION OF ANTI-BALLISTIC MISSILE SYTEMS

[A]

The Parties understand that, in addition to the ABM radars which may be deployed in accordance with subparagraph (a) of Article III of the Treaty, those non-phased-array ABM radars operational on the date of signature of the Treaty within the ABM system deployment area for defense of the national capital may be retained.

[B]

The Parties understand that the potential (the product of mean emitted power in watts and antenna area in square meters) of the smaller of the two large phased-array ABM radars referred to in subparagraph (b) of Article III of the Treaty is considered for purposes of the Treaty to be three million.

[C]

The Parties understand that the center of the ABM system deployment area centered on the national capital and the center of the ABM system deployment area containing ICBM silo launchers for each Party shall be separated by no less than thirteen hundred kilometers.

[D]

In order to insure fulfillment of the obligation not to deploy ABM systems and their components except as provided in Article III of the Treaty, the Parties agree that in the event ABM systems based on other physical principles and including components capable of substituting for ABM interceptor missiles, ABM launchers, or ABM radars are created in the future, specific limitations on such systems and their components would be subject to discussion in accordance with Article XIII and agreement in accordance with Article XIV of the Treaty.

[E]

The Parties understand that Article V of the Treaty includes obligations not to develop, test or deploy ABM interceptor missiles for the delivery by each ABM interceptor missile of more than one independently guided warhead.

[F]

The Parties agree not to deploy phased-array radars having a potential (the product of mean emitted power in watts and antenna area in square meters) exceeding three million, except as provided for in Articles III, IV and VI of the Treaty, or except for the purposes of tracking objects in outer space or for use as national technical means of verification.

[G]

The Parties understand that Article IX of the Treaty includes the obligation of the US and the USSR not to provide to other States technical descriptions or blue prints specially worked out for the construction of ABM systems and their components limited by the Treaty.

2. Common Understandings

Common understanding of the Parties on the following matters was reached during the negotiations:

A. Location of ICBM Defenses

The U.S. Delegation made the following statement on May 26, 1972:

Article III of the ABM Treaty provides for each side one ABM system deployment area centered on its national capital and one ABM system deployment area containing ICBM silo launchers. The two sides have registered agreement on the following statement: "The Parties understand that the center of the ABM system deployment area centered on the national capital and the center of the ABM system deployment area containing ICBM silo launchers for each Party shall be separated by no less than thirteen hundred kilometers." In this connection, the U.S. side notes that its ABM system deployment area for defense of ICBM silo launchers, located west of the Mississippi River, will be centered in the Grand Forks ICBM silo launcher deployment area. (See Agreed Statement [C].)

B. ABM Test Ranges

The U.S. Delegation made the following statement on April 26, 1972:

Article IV of the ABM Treaty provides that "the limitations provided for in Article III shall not apply to ABM systems or their components used for development or testing, and located within current or additionally agreed test ranges." We believe it would be useful to assure that there is no misunderstanding as to current ABM test ranges. It is our understanding that ABM test ranges encompass the area within which ABM components are located for test purposes. The current U.S. ABM test ranges are at White Sands, New Mexico, and at Kwajalein Atoll, and the current Soviet ABM test range is near Sary Shagan in Kazakhstan. We consider that non-phased array radars of types used for range safety or instrumentation purposes may be located outside of ABM test ranges. We interpret the reference in Article IV to "additionally agreed test ranges" to mean that ABM components will not be located at any other test ranges without prior agreement between our Governments that there will be such additional ABM test ranges.

On May 5, 1972, the Soviet Delegation stated that there was a common understanding on what ABM test ranges were, that the use of the types of non-ABM radars for range safety or instrumentation was not limited under the Treaty, that the reference in Article IV to "additionally agreed" test ranges was sufficiently clear, and that national means permitted identifying current test ranges.

C. Mobile ABM Systems

On January 29, 1972, the U.S. Delegation made the following statement:

Article V(1) of the Joint Draft Text of the ABM Treaty includes an undertaking not to develop, test, or deploy mobile land-based ABM systems and their components. On May 5, 1971, the U.S. side indicated that, in its view, a prohibition on deployment of mobile ABM systems and components would rule out the deployment of ABM launchers and radars which were not permanent fixed types. At that time, we asked for the Soviet view of this interpretation. Does the Soviet side agree with the U.S. side's interpretation put forward on May 5, 1971?

On April 13, 1972, the Soviet Delegation said there is a general common understanding on this matter.

D. Standing Consultative Commission

Ambassador Smith made the following statement on May 22, 1972:

The United States proposes that the sides agree that, with regard to initial implementation of the ABM Treaty's Article XIII on the Standing Consultative Commission (SCC) and of the consultation Articles to the Interim Agreement on offensive arms and the Accidents Agreement,[1] agreement establishing the SCC will be worked out early in the follow-on SALT negotiations; until that is completed, the following arrangements will prevail: when SALT is in session, any consultation desired by either side under these Articles can be carried out by the two SALT Delegations; when SALT is not in session, *ad hoc* arrangements for any desired consultations under these Articles may be made through diplomatic channels.

Minister Semenov replied that, on an *ad referendum* basis, he could agree that the U.S. statement corresponded to the Soviet understanding.

E. Standstill

On May 6, 1972, Minister Semenov made the following statement:

In an effort to accommodate the wishes of the U.S. side, the Soviet Delegation is prepared to proceed on the basis that the two sides will in fact observe the obligations of both the Interim Agreement and the ABM Treaty beginning from the date of signature of these two documents.

In reply, the U.S. Delegation made the following statement on May 20, 1972:

---

[1]See Article 7 of Agreement to Reduce the Risk of Outbreak of Nuclear War Between the United States of America and the Union of Soviet Socialist Republics, signed Sept. 30, 1971.

The U.S. agrees in principle with the Soviet statement made on May 6 concerning observance of obligations beginning from date of signature but we would like to make clear our understanding that this means that, pending ratification and acceptance, neither side would take any action prohibited by the agreements after they had entered into force. This understanding would continue to apply in the absence of notification by either signatory of its intention not to proceed with ratification or approval.

The Soviet Delegation indicated agreement with the U.S. statement.

3. Unilateral Statements

The following noteworthy unilateral statements were made during the negotiations by the United States Delegation:

A. Withdrawal from the ABM Treaty

On May 9, 1972, Ambassador Smith made the following statement:

The U.S. Delegation has stressed the importance the U.S. Government attaches to achieving agreement on more complete limitations on strategic offensive arms, following agreement on an ABM Treaty and on an Interim Agreement on certain measures with respect to the limitation of strategic offensive arms. The U.S. Delegation believes that an objective of the follow-on negotiations should be to constrain and reduce on a long-term basis threats to the survivability of our respective strategic retaliatory forces. The USSR Delegation has also indicated that the objectives of SALT would remain unfulfilled without the achievement of an agreement providing for more complete limitations on strategic offensive arms. Both sides recognize that the initial agreements would be steps toward the achievement of more complete limitations on strategic arms. If an agreement providing for more complete strategic offensive arms limitations were not achieved within five years, U.S. supreme interests could be jeopardized. Should that occur, it would constitute a basis for withdrawal from the ABM Treaty. The U.S. does not wish to see such a situation occur, nor do we believe that the USSR does. It is because we wish to prevent such a situation that we emphasize the importance the U.S. Government attaches to achievement of more complete limitations on strategic offensive arms. The U.S. Executive will inform the Congress, in connection with Congressional consideration of the ABM Treaty and the Interim Agreement, of this statement of the U.S. position.

B. Tested in ABM Mode

On April 7, 1972, the U.S. Delegation made the following statement:

Article II of the Joint Text Draft uses the term "tested in an ABM mode," in defining ABM components, and Article VI includes certain obligations concerning such testing. We believe that the sides should have a common understanding of this phrase. First, we would note that the testing provisions of the ABM Treaty are intended to apply to testing which occurs after the date of signature of the Treaty, and not to any testing which may have occurred in the past. Next, we would amplify the remarks we have made on this subject during the previous Helsinki phase by setting forth the objectives which govern the U.S. view on the subject, namely, while prohibiting testing of non-ABM components for ABM purposes: not to prevent testing of ABM components, and not to prevent testing of non-ABM components for non-ABM purposes. To clarify our interpretation of "tested in an ABM mode," we note that we would consider a launcher, missile or radar to be "tested in an ABM mode" if, for example, any of the following events occur: (1) a launcher is used to launch an ABM interceptor missile, (2) an interceptor missile is flight tested against a target vehicle which has a flight trajectory with characteristics of a strategic ballistic missile flight trajectory, or is flight tested in conjunction with the test of an ABM interceptor missile or an ABM radar at the same test range, or is flight tested to an altitude inconsistent with interception of targets against which air defenses are deployed, (3) a radar makes measurements on a cooperative target vehicle of the kind referred to in item (2) above during the reentry portion of its trajectory or makes measurements in conjunction with the test of an ABM interceptor missile or an ABM radar at the same test range. Radars used for purposes such as range safety or instrumentation would be exempt from application of these criteria.

C. No-Transfer Article of ABM Treaty

On April 18, 1972, the U.S. Delegation made the following statement:

In regard to this Article [IX], I have a brief and I believe self-explanatory statement to make. The U.S. side wishes to make clear that the provisions of this Article do not set a precedent for whatever provision may be considered for a Treaty on Limiting Strategic Offensive Arms. The question of transfer of strategic offensive arms is a far more complex issue, which may require a different solution.

D. No Increase in Defense of Early Warning Radars

On July 28, 1970, the U.S. Delegation made the following statement:

Since Hen House radars [Soviet ballistic missile early warning radars] can detect and track ballistic missile warheads at great distances, they have a significant ABM potential. Accordingly, the U.S. would regard any increase in the defenses of such radars by surface-to-air missiles as inconsistent with an agreement.

Protocol to the Treaty Between the United States of America and the Union of Soviet Socialist Republics on the Limitation of Anti-Ballistic Missile Systems

Signed at Moscow July 3, 1974
Ratification advised by U.S. Senate November 10, 1975
Ratified by U.S. President March 19, 1976
Instruments of ratification exchanged May 24, 1976
Proclaimed by U.S. President July 6, 1976
Entered into force May 24, 1976

The United States of America and the Union of Soviet Socialist Republics, hereinafter referred to as the Parties,

Proceeding from the Basic Principles of Relations between the United States of America and the Union of Soviet Socialist Republics signed on May 29, 1972,

Desiring to further the objectives of the Treaty between the United States of America and the Union of Soviet Socialist Republics on the Limitation of Anti-Ballistic Missile Systems signed on May 26, 1972, hereinafter referred to as the Treaty,

Reaffirming their conviction that the adoption of further measures for the limitation of strategic arms would contribute to strengthening international peace and security,

Proceeding from the premise that further limitation of anti-ballistic missile systems will create more favorable conditions for the completion of work on a permanent agreement on more complete measures for the limitation of strategic offensive arms,

Have agreed as follows:

Article I

1. Each Party shall be limited at any one time to a single area out of the two provided in Article III of the Treaty for deployment of anti-ballistic missile (ABM) systems or their components and accordingly shall not exercise its right to deploy an ABM system or its components in the second of the two ABM system deployment areas permitted by Article III of the Treaty, except as an exchange of one permitted area for the other in accordance with Article II of this Protocol.

2. Accordingly, except as permitted by Article II of this Protocol: the United States of America shall not deploy an ABM system or its components in the area centered on its capital, as permitted by Article III(a) of the Treaty, and the Soviet Union shall not deploy an ABM system or its components in the deployment area of intercontinental ballistic missile (ICBM) silo launchers as permitted by Article III(b) of the Treaty.

Article II

1. Each Party shall have the right to dismantle or destroy its ABM system and the components thereof in the area where they are presently deployed and to deploy an ABM system or its components in the alternative area permitted by Article III of the Treaty, provided that prior to initiation of construction, notification is given in accord

with the procedure agreed to in the Standing Consultative Commission, during the year beginning October 3, 1977 and ending October 2, 1978, or during any year which commences at five year intervals thereafter, those being the years for periodic review of the Treaty, as provided in Article XIV of the Treaty. This right may be exercised only once.

2. Accordingly, in the event of such notice, the United States would have the right to dismantle or destroy the ABM system and its components in the deployment area of ICBM silo launchers and to deploy an ABM system or its components in an area centered on its capital, as permitted by Article III(a) of the Treaty, and the Soviet Union would have the right to dismantle or destroy the ABM system and its components in the area centered on its capital and to deploy an ABM system or its components in an area containing ICBM silo launchers, as permitted by Article III(b) of the Treaty.

3. Dismantling or destruction and deployment of ABM systems or their components and the notification thereof shall be carried out in accordance with Article VIII of the ABM Treaty and procedures agreed to in the Standing Consultative Commission.

Article III

The rights and obligations established by the Treaty remain in force and shall be complied with by the Parties except to the extent modified by this Protocol. In particular, the deployment of an ABM system or its components within the area selected shall remain limited by the levels and other requirements established by the Treaty.

Article IV

This Protocol shall be subject to ratification in accordance with the constitutional procedures of each Party. It shall enter into force on the day of the exchange of instruments of ratification and shall thereafter be considered an integral part of the Treaty.

DONE at Moscow on July 3, 1974, in duplicate, in the English and Russian languages, both texts being equally authentic.

For the United States of America:

RICHARD NIXON

President of the United States of America

For the Union of Soviet Socialist Republics:

L. I. BREZHNEV

General Secretary of the Central Committee of the CPSU

Appendix C

Excerpt from President Reagan's March 23, 1983 Speech

Reprinted from *Weekly Compilation of Presidential Documents*, Washington, D.C.: Office of the Federal Register, National Archives and Records Services, General Services Administration, vol. 19, no. 13, 1984, pp. 447–448.

Excerpt from President Reagan's March 23, 1983 Speech

O ne of the most important contributions we can make is, of course, to lower the level of all arms, and particularly nuclear arms. We're engaged right now in several negotiations with the Soviet Union to bring about a mutual reduction of weapons. I will report to you a week from tomorrow my thoughts on that score. But let me just say, I'm totally committed to this course.

If the Soviet Union will join with us in our effort to achieve major arms reduction, we will have succeeded in stabilizing the nuclear balance. Nevertheless, it will still be necessary to rely on the specter of retaliation, on mutual threat. And that's a sad commentary on the human condition. Wouldn't it be better to save lives than to avenge them? Are we not capable of demonstrating our peaceful intentions by applying all our abilities and our ingenuity to achieving a truly lasting stability? I think we are. Indeed, we must.

After careful consultation with my advisers, including the Joint Chiefs of Staff, I believe there is a way. Let me share with you a vision of the future which offers hope. It is that we embark on a program to counter the awesome Soviet missile threat with measures that are defensive. Let us turn to the very strengths in technology that spawned our great industrial base and that have given us the quality of life we enjoy today.

What if free people could live secure in the knowledge that their security did not rest upon the threat of instant U.S. retaliation to deter a Soviet attack, that we could intercept and destroy strategic ballistic missiles before they reached our own soil or that of our allies?

I know this is a formidable, technical task, one that may not be accomplished before the end of this century. Yet, current technology has attained a level of sophistication where it's reasonable for us to begin this effort. It will take years, probably decades of effort on many fronts. There will be failures and setbacks, just as there will be successes and breakthroughs. And as we proceed, we must remain constant in preserving the nuclear deterrent and maintaining a solid capability for flexible response. But isn't it worth every investment necessary to free the world from the threat of nuclear war? We know it is.

In the meantime, we will continue to pursue real reductions in nuclear arms, negotiating from a position of strength that can be ensured only by modernizing our strategic forces. At the same time, we must take steps to reduce the risk of a conventional military conflict escalating to nuclear war by improving our non-nuclear capabilities.

America does possess—now—the technologies to attain very significant improvements in the effectiveness of our conventional, non-nuclear forces. Proceeding boldly with these new technologies, we can significantly reduce any incentive that the Soviet Union may have to threaten attack against the United States or its allies.

As we pursue our goal of defensive technologies, we recognize that our allies rely upon our strategic offense power to deter attacks against them. Their vital interests and ours are inextricably linked. Their safety and ours are one. And no change in technology can or will alter that reality. We must and shall continue to honor our commitments.

I clearly recognize that defensive systems have limitations and raise certain problems and ambiguities. If paired with offensive systems, they can be viewed as fostering an aggressive policy, and no one wants that. But with these considerations firmly in mind, I call upon the scientific community in our country, those who gave us nuclear weapons, to turn their great talents now to the cause of mankind and world peace, to give us the means of rendering these nuclear weapons impotent and obsolete.

Tonight, consistent with our obligations of the ABM treaty and recognizing the need for closer consultation with our allies, I'm taking an important first step. I am directing a comprehensive and intensive effort to define a long-term research and development program to begin to achieve our ultimate goal of eliminating the threat posed by strategic nuclear missiles. This could pave the way for arms control measures to eliminate the weapons themselves. We seek neither military superiority nor political advantage. Our only purpose—one all people share—is to search for ways to reduce the danger of nuclear war.

My fellow Americans, tonight we're launching an effort which holds the promise of changing the course of human history. There will be risks, and results take time. But I believe we can do it. As we cross this threshold, I ask for your prayers and your support.

Thank you, good night, and God bless you.

Index

About the Authors

Gary L. Guertner (B.A., M.A., University of Arizona; Ph.D., Claremont Graduate School) is professor of international relations at California State University, Fullerton. He held the Henry Stimson Chair of Political Science at the United States Army War College from 1981 to 1984, and served as Scholar-In-Residence at the United States Arms Control and Disarmament Agency in 1985. Dr. Guertner's articles on defense and foreign policy have appeared in *Foreign Policy, Political Science Quarterly, Orbis, Bulletin of the Atomic Scientists, Newsweek,* and numerous military journals.

Donald M. Snow (B.A., M.A., University of Colorado; Ph.D., Indiana University) is professor of political science and director of international studies at the University of Alabama. During 1985–1986, he served as Secretary of the Navy Senior Research Fellow and Professor of Management at the United States Naval War College. He has also served as visiting professor of national security affairs at the United States Air Command and Staff College. He is author or co-author of four other books and has had articles appear in *International Studies Quarterly, Political Science Quarterly, International Studies Notes, Bulletin of the Atomic Scientists, Arms Control Today, U.S. Naval War College Review, Parameters, Air University Review,* and *Christian Science Monitor.*